Frame Your Future

Building a Strategy to Lead You into a Life Full of God's Blessings

Dr. Willie L. Bradley Jr.

Copyright © 2020 by **Willie L. Bradley Jr.**

All rights reserved. No part of this publication may be reproduced, distributed, or transmitted in any form or by any means, without prior written permission.

Unless otherwise specified, all Scripture quotations are taken from the ESV® Bible (The Holy Bible, English Standard Version®). ESV® Text Edition: 2016. Copyright © 2001 by Crossway, a publishing ministry of Good News Publishers. The ESV® text has been reproduced in cooperation with and by permission of Good News Publishers. Unauthorized reproduction of this publication is prohibited. Used by permission. All rights reserved.

Scripture quotations marked (NIV) are taken from the Holy Bible, New International Version®, NIV® Copyright © 1973, 1978, 1984, 2011 by Biblica, Inc.® Used by permission. All rights reserved worldwide.

Renown Publishing

Frame Your Future / Willie L. Bradley Jr.
ISBN-13: 978-1-945793-99-8

This book is dedicated to the numerous loved ones, Anointed Remnant International Ministries congregants, and executive staff and covenant pastors of Anointed Remnant Global Assemblies who served as inspiration for the sermonic chapters.

This book is also dedicated to the stellar Dr. Marquita F. Davis—scholar, educator, county economic innovator, state finance director, and national strategic planner—whose mentorship, life example, and proactiveness served as a major rudder within the framework of my life.

Above all, there would be no work to dedicate without the divine guidance of God. To God be the glory!

CONTENTS

The Hidden Framework 3
Build Your Frame 9
The Seven P's, Factor #1: Prayerful— Trading Private Pain for Perfect Power 23
The Seven P's, Factor #2: Proficient— Empowered by Association 33
The Seven P's, Factor #3: Proactive— A Christian Champion's Mindset 45
The Seven P's, Factor #4: Prioritizing— What Are You Doing? 57
The Seven P's, Factor #5: Patient— Send Your Worries to God 67
The Seven P's, Factor #6: Productive— Doing the Most 77
The Seven P's, Factor #7: Professional— Independent from Outside Control 87
Don't Even Think About It 97
Wrong Place, Right Praise 107
Frustrated but Free 117
Not Totally Correct— But Totally Called 127
I'm Promoted 137
In It to Win It 145
A New Strategy 153
About the Author 155
Notes 156

INTRODUCTION

The Hidden Framework

God has a plan for every person. No one slips through the cracks. No one is forgotten. God has intricately woven a fabric that involves your thread, your life, so that a completed tapestry of His goodness might be seen by all.

God tells us repeatedly that He has a perfect plan for our lives. Why do so many of us not fulfill that perfect plan? Sometimes we simply don't know what those plans are. Sometimes we would rather settle for less. Sometimes we lose our focus and take our eyes off of Him.

We're like two old folks sitting on the front porch, watching the world pass by. The sounds of traffic, of birds, of children playing, of the floorboards creaking under the rocking chairs all beckon a conversation of better days gone by, the "good ol' days." But God has more for us in our good *current* days.

God has deep pockets full of blessings, and He longs to reach in and pull out a handful to sprinkle over our lives. Contrary to popular belief, God is not going to bless us if we use His goodness to sit on a porch, enjoying His blessings, while others labor for Him. We have a path and a part to play in positioning ourselves to receive those blessings. We need to frame our lives so that we walk in obedience to God's personalized, perfect plan.

From the very first moments of this world, God had a plan:

> *In the beginning, God created the heavens and the earth. The earth was without form and void, and darkness was over the face of the deep. And the Spirit of God was hovering over the face of the waters.*
>
> *And God said, "Let there be light," and there was light. And God saw that the light was good. And God separated the light from the darkness. God called the light Day, and the darkness he called Night. And there was evening and there was morning, the first day.*
> —**Genesis 1:1-5**

From the very first seconds of history, God was creating a framework. Many times, we hear messages from this passage as simply a story of creation, the first sin, and the fall of humanity from God. But this is a lesson from God on framework design to help us make sense of the world around us and make the most of our time on earth. When we look at creation in this light, the Word of God opens up new possibilities for our paths.

God created the different elements of the world in a specific order, giving us a powerful lesson on putting life's intricacies into place at different stages in our lives. God builds in a perfect order, sometimes slowly and sometimes quickly, so if you're living in the right framework, you will find yourself on the right path, ready to receive all the blessings He desires to give you.

What's a Framework?

When you look at a building, what do you see? You see the façade, the windows, the fixtures, the color of the exterior. Inside, furniture, paint, and decorations have been chosen to express the personality of the person to whom the building belongs. What you don't see are the joists supporting the floor, the load-bearing walls, the pipes, and the wires. What you don't see is the framework.

Online blogs are similar. When you first visit a website, the page is decorated to elicit a response from the visitor, whether to read further or to buy something. What you don't see is the framework holding up the website—the code, the algorithms, and the server where the data is saved.

In both cases, the better the framework, the better the building or website. While a framework is not showy or flashy, if it is not solid and the house or blog gets in a bit of trouble with storms or visitors, the whole thing comes crashing down.

Everything you do presents a framework for how you approach life. With the right framework, you can have success. Finding God's success requires a godly foundation. Otherwise you're wasting your time. True, there are many rich and popular people who don't know Christ. But we're not talking about worldly success. We're talking about souls saved, about personal joy, contentment of the highest order, and peace that fills the heart during the roughest storms. We're talking about the pleasures of singing God's praises and fellowshipping with God's people.

Success is watching your children and grandchildren follow the Lord. Success is watching lives change around you because of your walk with God. Success is learning something new about His character daily.

Success is a combination of key characteristics God wants us to demonstrate, such as being productive with the time, talents, resources, and passions He gives us; being professional in all of our dealings with others; developing proficiency and patience and prioritizing well in whatever we do; being proactive in obedience to God; and being prayerful in all things.

Being successful isn't merely about being blessed. It's about blessing others. These attributes are a bridge between the Bible and success, moving us forward into God's blessings. This success always starts with a powerful framework built on God.

How to Build the Framework

The success surrounding my God-given future was framed with what I define as *The Seven P Factors*: Prayer, Proactivity, Proficiency, Productivity, Professionalism, Prioritization, and Patience. Are you having difficulty with these principles? This book outlines the proper framework for a successful Christian life. Frame your future to be a reality, not a fantasy.

God has a plan for you, a framework around which to build your life. If you keep doing right, you will receive right things, and you will be building right. But you can't just sit and wait for God's blessings. You have a part to play in positioning yourself to receive these blessings. You've got a job to do, and this book will help explain what needs to be done to build a holy framework in your life.

In the following chapters, you'll discover how to choose and hone your vocabulary to reflect God, deal with pain, discern how associations with people and situations affect your framework, develop a Christian champion's mindset, know what to do in difficult situations, deal with worry and fear, please God, stay independent of negative outside influences, deal with temptation, keep your bad attitude in check, and develop the spiritual disciplines necessary to keep winning. At the end of each chapter, a workbook section will provide you with specific steps for building your framework.

It's time to start framing your future. The stronger your framework, the more God can bless you. If you don't start framing now, your future will simply pass you by, and you'll be in a void that God never wanted for you. In order to live the blessed life that God has prepared for you, frame your future according to God's personalized plan.

Let's start building the frame.

CHAPTER ONE

Build Your Frame

Helen Keller hardly knew what it was to see or hear.[1] Deaf and blind from an illness she suffered as a toddler, she experienced little of the world around her. She couldn't communicate, she couldn't observe the world around her, and she seemingly had no way to function or contribute.

She became a wild child. Her life was one of trying to get her needs met. Hunger, thirst, anger, and frustration were her only experiences. She knew nothing outside of the world she could feel with her limited senses.

What future did Helen have? How could she plan, grow, and build? All she knew was the trial and error from her past. How could she learn about God or obedience or so many other things we take for granted, like manners and kindness?

God began to lay His astonishing framework when He led a gifted and extremely patient teacher named Annie Sullivan into Helen's life. One day, when working with Helen by an outdoor well, Annie poured water over Helen's hand and signed the letters *w-a-t-e-r* into her other palm. Helen understood. She knew one word; perhaps she could learn more.

Annie showed Helen how to communicate by signs, created by pressing her fingers into other people's palms. It was in that moment that Helen began to build a framework that would construct her life, a life that ultimately changed the world. Helen Keller's influence cannot be quantified.

In many ways, we all are like Helen Keller: we often find ourselves confused, not understanding the world around us. We need someone—*Someone*—to help us build a frame that will serve as a lifelong scaffold of understanding and growth, like the one Annie Sullivan offered Helen.

> *My frame was not hidden from you, when I was being made in secret, intricately woven in the depths of the earth.*
> **—Psalm 139:15**

Helen Keller's life, before she awakened to a bigger world, was one of selfish desires built upon looking to the past. It was a life of pure cause and effect. If she exhibited being upset, she would be fed. If she cried, she would be checked for an injury. If she needed anything, she had to guess at how to communicate that need.

There was no way she could plan for the future, brace for the unknown, or guess what was coming next. All she knew was what had sometimes worked in the past.

Framing Forward

You can't plan for the future if your eyes are fixed on the past. If you live a life purely based on the effects of your own instinctual behavior, if you aren't intentional or strategic with the framework of your life, you will live in a small, selfish world like Helen Keller's world before she met Annie.

If you continue to do only what you've been doing, you'll always get the same results. It's by actively searching the Scriptures, learning about God's character, and obeying that you will be able to build a framework that allows you to embrace the future.

We use the word *frame* for so many things that it's impossible to list them all here. A picture frame offers a stiff enclosure that focuses the viewer's eyes to a specific theme or point, colored in such a way as to draw out aspects the artist wants seen first.

There are also frames of mind, frames for eyeglasses, and the house frames we talked about earlier. We pass through door frames. Many people discuss time frames, such as the nine months before birth, the four years until graduation, and the thirty years before the home mortgage is paid off.

What do all frames have in common? They offer helpful guidelines, boundaries, goals, clarity, structure, and strength.

Have you ever thought of your future in terms of framing? To look at the future, let's again look as far into the past as we can go:

> *In the beginning, God created the heavens and the earth. The earth was without form and void, and darkness was over the face of the deep. And the Spirit of God was hovering over the face of the waters.*
>
> *And God said, "Let there be light," and there was light. And God saw that the light was good. And God separated the light from the darkness. God called the light Day, and the darkness he called Night. And there was evening and there was morning, the first day.*
> —***Genesis 1:1–5***

When God created the world, He didn't just create

human beings and hope for the best. He built a framework that would support the future, using both His authority and His power. What if God had skipped the first day? We would still be in the dark. How about a different day? What bit of creation could you live without? Maybe the moon and the stars? We could skip those tides and the light at night. We don't need stars to navigate ships or to create the perfect gravitational pull so that our solar system is stable, right?

God created the perfect framework, and we also need to build a framework for our future by looking ahead and not behind. Building on what we've learned from the past is valuable, but living in the past isn't.

We all have painful collections of hurt and trauma. Lives, bodies, and hearts have been injured and sometimes broken. We've lost jobs, struggled in our marriages, and suffered the deaths of close relatives and friends.

Losing a loved one is a painful ordeal, and moving ahead by building a framework under tragic conditions is difficult enough. But how do you move forward when a spouse commits suicide? When a child develops cancer? When a granddaughter is injured in a car accident?

What about your own health? What if your emotions tumble like a waterfall and crash into rocks, and you have no idea why?

How do you build a future when your past is littered with the remains of brokenness?

Breathe!

Just take one breath. And while you're taking that breath, when you're ready, plan for the next breath. And then you'll need another. Perhaps a bite of food now. Slowly, easy does it. Sometimes the food doesn't stay down. Sometimes it does. Breathe. Yes, it may hurt to breathe, but the pain will fade away.

Jesus also experienced hurt. He lost close friends. His father died. He knew of His own death, how He would die. Jesus has a hand on your back when you're curled in a fetal position due to unexplainable heartache.

God will help you build, and while you learn from tragedy, God doesn't want you to live as a victim. As you heal, ever so slowly building a framework of self-care—eating, sleeping, talking with friends and family—you will encounter others who have similar struggles, and you'll be able to offer framed advice. Because you have found that survival is attainable, you now have the building blocks to help others.

Living in the past, however, helps no one. Learn, then focus on rebuilding your framework. This is key to healing. Letting go of those things that trouble us will only happen as we look and walk directly toward Christ and then start building a framework.

The Dos and Don'ts of Building Frameworks

There's a long list of *don'ts* to follow when building a frame.

Don't covet other people's frames. To begin with, as you build the frame for your own life, make sure that you're building *your* frame for *your* life. Don't copy or even peek at other frames. Don't tell people what to do with their frames or mention how they should build them. Don't try to convince others to build your frame for you. Build your own frame. Keep your vision locked on to your framework, and the future of what you build will be secure and successful.

Don't live a sin-filled life. Romans 13:13 says, "Let us walk properly as in the daytime, not in orgies and drunkenness, not in sexual immorality and sensuality, not in quarreling and jealousy." Build a frame that maximizes daylight and sunshine and warmth, not one that requires drawn shades, closed doors, and locks to keep the sin hidden away.

Simply put, stay focused on what Christ has laid out before you. The Apostle Paul wrote, "But one thing I do: forgetting what lies behind and straining forward to what lies ahead, I press on toward the goal for the prize of the upward call of God in Christ Jesus" (Philippians 3:13b–14). As Paul penned these words, he had to focus on putting his past behind him. He had played a key part in finding and killing Christians, something he had to come to terms with, then put behind him. He had to obey the Lord's leading in giving Christ-followers time to learn to trust his new framework. This couldn't be rushed any more than healing and dealing with our pasts can be rushed.

But Paul also needed to keep his eyes on God. He needed to do precisely what the Spirit led him to do precisely when and how he was led. His focus in every hour was listening to and obeying the Lord. God was using him to do something that had never been done before: planting churches in the name of Jesus across the known world. Whether he was aware of it or not, Paul was building a framework for missions that would last for millennia. He was putting the past behind him and pressing on.

Paul was building a frame for success. He was *doing* the right things as well as *not doing* the unhelpful things. The list of *dos* is more fun. Write this list down and craft a plan for following through.

Make a list of words that define you. List the good and the bad. Start with the fruit of the Spirit: "But the fruit of the Spirit is love, joy, peace, patience, kindness, goodness, faithfulness, gentleness, self-control; against such things there is no law" (Galatians 5:22–23).

Are you prone to jealousy? Write that down. Do you like to laugh and tell jokes, making others laugh as well? Add it to the list. How about skills like singing, writing, and drawing? Jot those down. Do you love to encourage people? Are you quiet? Are you loud? Do you love to read? Do you like tinkering with car engines? All of it is important.

Ask your close friends to describe you. One woman struggled with illness and pain all her life, but she still found ways to contribute at church and in a local school. Despite being frail and some days unable to rise from bed, she was able to make a small difference. When she asked her friends to describe her, they said she was the strongest person they knew, shocking her. Question your close friends and write down what they say.

Rework your thoughts and create your own description of yourself. Keep this for moments when you feel lost and need time to think over your framework. Who you are is how God built you, from your likes and dislikes to your hopes and dreams. God made you unlike anyone else, and the frame you build will be individual to you.

Know what you want. Take time to think about your desires before those desires give way to opportunity. Proficiency will reveal itself when preparation meets opportunity. Despite your strengths, if you have not prepared for the opportunities that may arise, then fear and discontent will set in. You will unquestionably throw away perfect opportunities. At the very least, you're wasting time. At the worst, you're sitting on a rocker, watching the world go by.

You must have a goal, a target to aim for. Otherwise, you'll be tossed around by the waves of life (Ephesians 4:14). Determine what you want in this life. You can't build a frame if you keep changing your mind and starting over. Knowing what you desire will eliminate wrong turns and delayed success.

Have realistic goals. Every framework is initiated from a blueprint. It's constructed from a basic plan, design, or proposal. When outlining your goals, maintain a blueprint focus of the process and steps.

In Habakkuk, the prophet wrote that the Lord

instructed him to "write the vision; make it plain on tablets, so he may run who reads it" (Habakkuk 2:2). The tablets provided a practical way to make realistic goals. Grab a pad and pencil and start writing out some goals for yourself.

A realistic goal means having a workable and practical idea of what can be achieved or expected. Create a mental picture of your desire for life and outline the steps that will be required. You can then implement the design and make adjustments to stabilize your future goals. You will need perseverance to give daily effort, endure short-lived delays, and persist even when you can't see the finish line.

You can't run a ten-mile race if you have no desire to run or have physical limitations. If God lays it on your heart to start a group at church to run a race at the end of the year and you love running, then dream big. Write down your goal and dream big. You know what it involves. But if you hate jogging, why get tangled up in something you have no idea about? Know what the outcome should look like.

Think through the pitfalls that could lead to failure. Wanting to tithe but having no way to make money will lead to failure. Back to the example of jogging, if you attempt to run ten miles on the first day of your training, you're asking for failure—or, should I say, cardiac arrest.

You'll need to change your viewpoint to ensure success. If you can't tithe, consider a service, such as cleaning the church. Monetary tithes and serving with your time are equally important. If you can't jog, but you want to be involved in running, can you coach? Can you bring water and be an encourager? There are so many ways to get involved. It just takes some thinking as you build the framework for the future.

But seek first the kingdom of God and his righteousness, and all these things will be added to you.
—**Matthew 6:33**

When building a framework for your future, seek first the kingdom of God. Keep looking to Him. He will supply the desires, the focus, and the care you need as you build. If you find yourself stumbling, make sure that you're putting God first. Keep going back to Scripture, to the spiritual landmarks in your life, to the dreams you wrote down when they were fresh, to the beginnings of your frame. Go back to the original blueprint that the Lord gave you.

Building a frame for life will include some difficulties, but the end result will be worth it. Keep reading to discover some potential stumbling blocks as well as benefits of staying focused on God as you build your future.

WORKBOOK

Chapter One Questions

Question: What does it mean to build a framework for your life? If you are not intentional in building your framework, what sort of default framework is likely to arise?

_____

_____

_____

_____

_____

_____

_____

_____

_____

_____

_____

_____

Question: What should the role of your past be in building your framework for the future? What are some common pitfalls that come from focusing too much on the past?

_____
_____
_____
_____
_____
_____
_____
_____
_____
_____

Question: How should seeking God's kingdom first influence each aspect of your framework?

_____
_____
_____
_____
_____
_____

_____

_____

_____

_____

_____

Action: Grab a notebook or journal and start on the *dos* in this chapter. Write out words, thoughts, goals, and ideas related to your frame.

Chapter One Notes

CHAPTER TWO

The Seven P's, Factor #1: Prayerful— Trading Private Pain for Perfect Power

But he said to me, "My grace is sufficient for you, for my power is made perfect in weakness."
—*2 Corinthians 12:9a*

Pain, in many forms, can keep you from building a framework. But does it have to? Many people live with secrets and private pain; however, not everyone is held back by that pain.

John Corcoran, a renowned educator, continues to baffle his peers to this day. After obtaining his bachelor's degree, he spent nearly seventeen years as a teacher—and due to learning difficulties, he did it all without knowing how to read. Only his wife knew his secret.

In an interview, he explained:

> I had a certain confidence that I could look normal on the

outside to those around me, but I never did feel normal on the inside. I love the truth and I love to seek the truth, so I always felt like my deceit was tripping me up as an educator. It was a constant obstacle to deal with.[2]

Like John Corcoran, many of us deal with secret obstacles that attempt to keep us from experiencing God's perfect plan for our lives.

If a carpenter is building a frame for a house but doesn't even know where to begin, there might be a problem. Or maybe he's too weak to lift a hammer. Then what is he to do? What if an interior decorator is color-blind? These obstacles take some creative thinking, but they don't fall into the category of sin.

Unexpected pain and unplanned secrets hinder our ability to work. Perhaps, for example, a wedding planner is supposed to plan a wedding, but her husband just handed her divorce papers.

Pain can be of our own making or the making of others. Either way, we're forced to deal with it. The pain has to be addressed in order for the frame to be built with integrity. Pain does not have to define us or hold us back from fulfilling God's call on our lives.

Pain and Coping: Bringing Us Closer to God

If you get to know people well enough, you learn that they're dealing with pain they don't want others to know about. Everyone deals with private pain, whether it be sin, loss, disappointment, or illness. The answer of how to cope with this pain lies within our strong framework foundation. We need to let our pain push us into the strong, understanding arms of Jesus, who stands ready to receive and heal.

When you have private pain, to whom can you turn? Whom can you talk with who will not tell others or worry?

Why is private pain such a big deal? Because these problems can be embarrassing and tragic. A woman was abused as a girl, and it was covered up. Now she overeats to hide the pain. A man is addicted to gambling and steals to feed his habit. A woman receives the final word that she'll never get pregnant, and she pushes God away in anger. A man is unhappy with his marriage and turns to pornography, and now he is addicted.

You may be dealing with a situation just as difficult. Private pain and unhealthy coping mechanisms are weakening people spiritually. The only chance to find healing is to turn our pain over to God first. We are not to worry about it, and we aren't simply to jump in and do whatever it takes to fix it. We are to give it to God, run to Him in prayer, and ask Him to deal with our pain. Then He will direct the next steps.

Perhaps the abused woman is to go to the police. The woman who can't get pregnant is to come to peace with this and other feelings of inadequacy so that she can help others. The man's problems with addiction might lead him to professional groups for accountability.

God designed humans to function as whole beings: spirit, soul, and body. The spirit allows God-consciousness, the soul self-consciousness, and the body world-consciousness. Sin breaks and fragments our wholeness.

As Paul wrote, "Now may the God of peace himself sanctify you completely, and may your whole spirit and soul and body be kept blameless at the coming of our Lord Jesus Christ" (1 Thessalonians 5:23). The only way to find perfect peace is to start with God and follow Him through the recovery process.

The Next Steps

Even if you are a victim of abuse and you contact the authorities, and the abuser stops hurting you and others, there's still a problem. The pain still lingers. The shame and confusion don't go away.

Addicts sometimes feel drawn to their old sins. Sometimes they feel the need to gamble or return to their previous actions. When an infertile woman sees children playing, won't she still feel the pang of her inability to conceive?

What's causing the private pain? After giving your pain to the Lord, buy a journal and start making notes. Take note of the pain and suffering and search for the real reasons. Does the pain come from a feeling of inadequacy? From a longing for love? From the violation of your privacy?

Notice and write down what you do to cope. Do you shop? Do you overeat? Do you try to take on extra work to make up for the sin? Pain is cyclical: guilt, innocence, sadness, semi-joy, and then the pain intrudes again. You can break this cycle by reading through your journal, noticing patterns, and breaking the cycle at any point. Recognizing the cycle and calling out to God for help and forgiveness is the best way to fix a broken or bent frame.

God offers incredible comfort, not just with the big things but with everyday life as well. Offer up the sins that you may think are smaller. Start with the little things so that the big ones aren't so daunting. As you practice surrendering and submitting in the little issues and you experience God's faithfulness and blessing in those areas, you will get more comfortable surrendering the major issues. Give it all to Him. He is faithful to forgive and to give you a fresh start (1 John 1:9; Lamentations 3:22–23).

Once you have the peace and comfort of forgiveness, there is strength to draw on when you're tempted to doubt, to sin again, or just to sit down in the face of your obstacles. You will need strength to deal with all the private pains, those that are based in sin and those that aren't.

When you are forgiven and filled with strength, your

new mindset is one of refreshed endurance. The success gives you perfect power and perfect peace, a stark contrast with the anxiety and trouble that have been plaguing you.

Perfection and strength lie in ensuring that you take these steps with God so that you experience forgiveness and power. By dealing with our private pain in harmful ways, we are looking outside of God's framework for our lives and trying to find life in sources that aren't part of our framework at all. If we look outside of God's frame first, the result will always be pain.

The solution is to repair and build our framework in healthy ways, with the Lord at the drawing board every step of the way. Build your life framework free of private pain and let God strengthen you to overcome every obstacle of sin.

WORKBOOK

Chapter Two Questions

Question: What are some examples of private pain from your own life or the lives of your loved ones? (If you are in a group, no one should be pressured to answer this question aloud.) Why does private pain have such a hold over us? How can sharing that pain in a safe place or with a trustworthy person bring freedom and healing?

_____

_____

_____

_____

_____

_____

_____

_____

_____

_____

Question: What are some common coping mechanisms? What are your personal coping mechanisms for dealing with your own pain and/or guilt? How do pain and coping mechanisms create an endless cycle?

_____

_____

_____

_____

_____

_____

_____

_____

_____

Question: How can you allow God to bring comfort and forgiveness to you and break your cycle of pain and coping?

_____

_____

_____

_____

_____

_____

_____

_____

_____

_____

_____

Action: Support groups, lay and professional counseling, and caregiving ministries, such as Stephen Ministry, provide supportive environments for people to share painful life experiences. Depending on where you are in your journey, consider availing yourself of one of these resources or training to become a Christian caregiver who can help others in dealing with their pain.

Chapter Two Notes

CHAPTER THREE

The Seven P's, Factor #2: Proficient— Empowered by Association

Lee, an energetic teenager, ran with a group of boys who were in trouble more often than not. *Mischievous* would be a nice word for the crew. Prior to 1990, the American school system's correctional method for such boys often involved a paddle. In the South, back in the day, a fight between naughty boys would result in a paddling by the school principal.

One day, Lee was sick and couldn't make it to class. Ironically, at school, the group of boys hassled another young man, and they eventually found themselves dangling the lad by his ankles from the library balcony. They were caught by the principal, and swift justice came in the form of a paddling.

The next day, when Lee returned to school, he was called into the principal's office, where an angry paddle met his backside. Lee was understandably upset. "What did I do?" he asked.

The principal towered over him. "If you had been in school yesterday, you would have been involved in hanging that poor boy over the balcony. You know it's true. That's why you were paddled."

Whether you feel that Lee's punishment was fair or not, the point is that his associations created a framework in his life that encouraged sin. There was no doubt in anyone's mind, including in Lee's, that he would have been involved.

Your associations help to shape your framework. When you look through your framework, whom do you see? Do you see God, or do you see the crew with which you've been spending your time?

Guilty or Successful by Association

Guilt by association is a legal term that means there may not be evidence that someone is guilty, but because the person with whom he or she is associating is an offender, they are both guilty. Both are held responsible.

When we build a frame, we need to build good associations into it. We need to associate with light and goodness, or we'll find ourselves in a frame marked by the shadows of others' darkness. Our associations have power in our lives, so we must choose them wisely.

> *...for God gave us a spirit not of fear but of power and love and self-control.*
> —2 Timothy 1:7

Just by being with the wrong person at the wrong time, you can find yourself in a world of trouble. You can get in trouble with law enforcement because you loaned the getaway car to the thief, even though you never robbed anyone. You can spend too much time with big spenders and find yourself in deep debt, trying to keep up. You can stay silent when off-color jokes make the rounds at work, and your conscience and reputation will suffer. Even as schoolchildren, some of us got in trouble because we passed notes from one class clown to another.

Our spiritual lives are no different. Too often, we associate ourselves with people and situations that don't honor God, and then we wonder what's wrong with our lives. We're not building a framework pleasing to Him.

Empowering means giving authority or power to someone or something in our lives. God has given us the power and authority to choose for ourselves, yet we oftentimes allow negative associations to have control over us.

When athletes grind out practice in the heat of the day, they grow weary and dehydrated. Many times, they're shuttled to the sidelines, where trainers provide replenishing fluids to restore their finishing power.

The athletes choose to hand authority over to someone who has life-giving power. We need to do the same by giving authority to Jesus. When we do that, He empowers us with a healthy dose of the Holy Spirit.

In today's world, we don't talk much about the Holy Spirit, but Jesus couldn't stop talking about Him. John 14:26 is a good example: "But the Helper, the Holy Spirit, whom the Father will send in my name, he will teach you all things and bring to your remembrance all that I have said to you." Jesus was talking about replenishment. If you're looking for power and success by association, look no further; you've found it. It's in the Holy Spirit.

If you're filled with the Holy Spirit instead of selfish desires and sin, you are free to build the framework God has for you. As you set goals, reflect on the past, but focus on your future as you walk forward with supernatural wisdom, strength, and assurance.

Three Associations of the Holy Spirit

When you're looking directly to God and you're filled

with the Holy Spirit, you'll be led to three different associations that will help, not hinder, you in building your framework: people, activities, and plans.

People

The Holy Spirit draws you to other believers. You will find them at church or in small groups. Friendships will form and blossom over breakfasts, Bible studies, and fellowship opportunities. You will find fellow Christians when you serve others—when you gather and distribute food for the poor, paint an elderly person's house, or clean the rooms of those with disabilities.

But what if you've got three buddies over, and between the three, they have twelve felonies? They're unrepentant, self-centered, and angry. When they walk out of your house, the police are watching.

Or you've got three ladies over who instantly start complaining about their husbands. Then they talk about what they'd like to do with the new young man down the street. They tear down the people they know, telling stories that may or may not be true.

Are these the people you want influencing your thoughts, goals, and behavior? Are these the people you want to influence your family? Do you want them to be part of your framework building? Successful associations help to build a successful framework.

Participate in Positive Events

Put yourself in situations that build up your frame, not ones that tear it down. Put yourself in places where the language, topics of conversation, and activities contribute to growth. Put yourself in contexts where there's encouragement, laughter, biblical perspectives and worldviews, truth, and compassion for others. Associate with light, and your own frame will be strengthened.

Activities

Jesus said, "Behold, I have given you authority to tread on serpents and scorpions, and over all the power of the enemy, and nothing shall hurt you" (Luke 10:19).

What activities are you involved in? Are you building your frame, or are you doing things that tear it down? I knew a man who said that if he was the smartest man in the room, he was in the wrong room. His focus on building his frame was to get wisdom from everyone he could. So he found men of God, the wisest and the most thoughtful, and he stayed nearby to watch and listen.

Are you spending all your time playing video games or binge-watching television? Those things don't build frames. You need to take part in activities that will take you somewhere, not mire you in the world's thinking.

Many times, it's difficult to choose good activities because it takes willpower. When we're tired or depressed, our willpower is nearly gone. Taking care of the bodies God gave us is important. Get enough sleep. Eat healthy foods. Exercise regularly. Care for others. Walk with friends. Go to church. Serve others. All these things are good for you; they strengthen your willpower and your framework.

Plans

You need to have a plan for your life! When someone asks, "What are you going to do with your life?" don't brush off the question. The question is serious, and if you've never put thought into it before, now's the time. What are you going to do with your life? You need a plan.

What does it mean to associate yourself with a power-based plan? When you're working on a plan for your life, make sure that you're grounded in the Word. Make your life one that is bolstered by prayer and devotions. Start building your plan and framework while you're going to church and talking with Christian friends. Bible study is a great time to chat with others about your plans.

Be wise about whom you talk to when discussing your plans. Some people have quit on God or plans for themselves and want everyone else to quit as well. If they're discouraging you instead of showing wise advice, then don't let them have input or influence over this part of your life.

Remember, we are to "seek first the kingdom of God and his righteousness, and all these things will be added to you" (Matthew 6:33). When you start there, the Holy Spirit will direct you forward.

Focus on God

In Jeremiah 38, we read that Jeremiah was preaching the Word of God, warning the Israelites that their sins were catching up with them and punishment was on its way. Angry at Jeremiah for being right, the officials marched to the king and demanded that Jeremiah be put to death. The people tossed him into a pit.

Sometimes you can't give people the Word. First, they don't want it, and second, they won't listen anyway. But Jeremiah didn't give up. Even though he was tossed into a pit and no one wanted him, he didn't give up. Why? He loved the ungodly people, yes, but stronger than his love for them was his focused vision of God and the framework He had built. Jeremiah simply could not help himself; he had to speak as the Lord directed him: "...his word is in my heart like a fire, a fire shut up in my bones. I am weary of holding it in; indeed, I cannot" (Jeremiah 20:9 NIV).

When you focus on God, you will associate with godly people, godly situations, godly activities, and godly plans.

If God isn't in them, they're not good for the future framework you're building.

The Holy Spirit helps you to hear from God and then gives you power, strength, and confidence to follow Him. You access the Holy Spirit by associating with the things and people of God, such as Scripture, prayer, and the body of Christ. Dig into His Word and surround yourself with His people and His purposes. When you make poor decisions—because we all do—refocus on God, and He will help you turn around, back to His frame for your life. Framing your life with godly associations is vital for your future.

WORKBOOK

Chapter Three Questions

Question: How can the people with whom you associate make or break you? With whom do you spend the most time? Do they have the sort of attitude, lifestyle, and walk with God that you want to characterize your own life in five years?

_____

_____

_____

_____

_____

_____

_____

_____

_____

_____

Question: What sort of people will the Holy Spirit draw you toward for close friendship? What is the difference between isolating yourself and protecting yourself? How can you influence lost people for Christ without allowing them to influence you away from Him?

_____

_____

_____

_____

_____

_____

_____

_____

_____

_____

Question: Give examples of situations and activities that the Holy Spirit will lead you away from. What are some situations and activities that the Holy Spirit may prompt you to be involved in? What principles should guide you regarding activities that are not inherently good or bad (entertainment, hobbies)?

_____

_____

_____

_____
_____
_____
_____
_____
_____
_____
_____

Action: For a week, keep track of all your time. Make a list of every influence in your life (people, TV, music, church, etc.) and how much time you spend with each. Have you empowered these people and things to direct your life? Are they influencing you more than the Holy Spirit is, or is He using them in your life?

Chapter Three Notes

CHAPTER FOUR

The Seven P's, Factor #3: Proactive— A Christian Champion's Mindset

What's a champion's secret? Coffee? Maybe it's a workout schedule or being blessed with special talents. Something sets a champion apart from the rest of us. What if I told you that you, too, can have the mindset of a champion, no coffee or working out necessary?

Consider the story of David and Goliath in 1 Samuel 17. Can you imagine being too young and small to lift a sword or wear armor? Your father tells you to take food to your older brothers, and you pause at the edge of a dusty plain, two battle lines shimmering in the sun. The hot air blows through your hair, and you grip the basket.

What are you feeling? A sense of awe? Apprehension? People kill here and die here! Do you want to run? Do you want to make sure that your brothers are safe? The men are dressed for battle, and a cry goes up from the enemy lines. You'd best hurry.

An enormous spear lands between the battle lines. As you step into the middle of the battlefield, you see a towering giant of a man. What is controlling your mindset?

Will you cower down or champion up? Your framework will direct your mindset and actions.

You leave your provisions with the commissary. Then, finding your brothers, you yell out a greeting, just as the giant also calls out. His voice is as large as he is:

> *"Why have you come out to draw up for battle? Am I not a Philistine, and are you not servants of Saul? Choose a man for yourselves, and let him come down to me. If he is able to fight with me and kill me, then we will be your servants. But if I prevail against him and kill him, then you shall be our servants and serve us." And the Philistine said, "I defy the ranks of Israel this day. Give me a man, that we may fight together."*
> —*1 Samuel 17:8-10*

Did that giant just defy God? Anger surges through your heart. You look at your brothers, expecting them to be reaching for their swords. Instead, they've taken a step back. They're frightened? You look around and see that everyone is fearful. What is this? Isn't God on their side?

You can't hold it back any longer: "For who is this uncircumcised Philistine, that he should defy the armies of the living God?" (1 Samuel 17:26b).

Your brothers tell you to be quiet and explain that the man is ten feet, six inches tall and a deadly killer. His spear is a massive, sharpened beam, and anyone who could get close enough to swing a sword at him would be crushed with a single blow.

Then you learn that the king is offering a generous reward to the Israelite who defeats this giant: a royal daughter in marriage, wealth, and exemption from taxes. A runner pauses and turns directly to you: "The king wants to talk to you."

You proceed nervously to the king. He's trying to lead a country in war, but he pauses in the battle because he wants to talk to *you*.

The royal tent reflects a battle command, with flags and banners, arms, and soldiers who look surprisingly fresh. Have they fought at all? You're led inside.

The king stands before you, and again, you can't keep from staring. These men should be stepping into battle against this giant, Goliath. If they aren't going to do it, then it's up to you: "Let no man's heart fail because of him. Your servant will go and fight with this Philistine" (1 Samuel 17:32).

To your surprise, the king takes you seriously, but he mentions how young you are in contrast to Goliath, who has been training to fight since he was your age while you've been tending sheep all your life.

But you have killed your share of beasts. Lions and bears constantly prey on the flock, but you've used your sling to kill them all. Your frame was uniquely designed by God in preparation for this situation. Besides, you've got something the king has not mentioned: the power of God.

The king hesitates before agreeing. He pulls out his armor, which is far too large for you. You are left alone to prepare. With a staff in one hand, you go down to a stream and collect five smooth stones. You place the stones in your pouch next to your sling.

Are you scared? Are you praying? Are you determined? Yes, yes, and yes. Your framework is foundationally established.

When you walk through the battle line, are you jeered or cheered? Do you even hear?

When the giant sees you, he throws insults, but you return them with a warning about how God will protect you and the Israelites.

The completion of your victory is aligned with David's story in the Bible:

> *When the Philistine arose and came and drew near to meet David, David ran quickly toward the battle line to meet the Philistine. And David put his hand in his bag and took out a stone and slung it and struck the Philistine on his forehead. The stone sank into his forehead, and he fell on his face to the ground.*
>
> *So David prevailed over the Philistine with a sling and with a stone, and struck the Philistine and killed him. There was no sword in the hand of David. Then David ran and stood over the Philistine and took his sword and drew it out of its sheath and killed him and cut off his head with it. When the Philistines saw that their champion was dead, they fled. And the men of Israel and Judah rose with a shout and pursued the Philistines as far as Gath and the gates of Ekron, so that the wounded Philistines fell on the way from Shaaraim as far as Gath and Ekron.*
> —**1 Samuel 17:48-52**

The Heart of a Champion

God still has champions like David. If you say you're a Christian, then you're a chosen champion here on earth. You might not feel like one or be prepared, but just like God prepared David, who was delivering lunch and ended up delivering Israel, God is also preparing you and positioning you for battle.

Often the label *Christian* is applied to a believer who has no intention of going into battle for Christ. At times, Christians are seen as lonely and weak, powerless to stop the devil unless God works a last-minute miracle by distracting the evil. But as He was with David, God is on our side, and we're to stop evil in its tracks.

Merriam-Webster defines *champion* as "a person who has defeated or surpassed all rivals, one that does battle for another."[3]

Champions have three historic components in their framework:

1. *Champions don't become champions without a fight.* Champions defeat the enemy. They actively pursue the battle against evil, taking on the fight against the enemy instead of cowering in avoidance of the fight.

Football players get injured. The battle on the gridiron is a fight for the ball, and pain is a part of the game. If you're on the field, you're going to get hit, even if you're a punter.

The same is true with the Christian life. When on the playing field of this world, it's reasonable to expect injuries. When you run up against something bigger than you, you may get knocked down and hurt, but you learn to get back up and keep playing. When you're hit hard, you recover and then play as you're able.

2. *Champions don't give up.* The first time you're struck, it's a shock. Many crawl away and nurse their injuries, never to return to the fight. Champions return to the fight, taking all they've learned to battle smarter and stronger. Champions never quit. They keep going.

3. *Challenges will come.* Championship stories always include obstacles. When the hero overcomes, we're inspired. Why does the champion's journey inspire us? Because we want to be like the hero. We want to inspire others, to overcome challenges, to see what will happen if we never give up.

Challenges make champions. The champion mindset is always forward-focused, walking forward with God and not retreating, knowing that the battle belongs to the Lord (1 Samuel 17:47).

David and Goliath

Now that you know what makes up a champion, let's look again at the story of David and his battle with

Goliath.

When Goliath saw David for the first time, the Philistine threw an insult: "Come to me, and I will give your flesh to the birds of the air and to the beasts of the field" (1 Samuel 17:44).

David replied, "You come to me with a sword and with a spear and with a javelin, but I come to you in the name of the LORD of hosts, the God of the armies of Israel, whom you have defied" (1 Samuel 17:45).

David directed the battle and the giant toward God. Instead of David claiming victory because of his amazing swing-arm skills, he knew that the credit belonged to God alone.

Satan always attempts to intimidate with threats, but Christians shall simply reply, "Be gone, Satan!" (Matthew 4:10).

Another aspect of champions is fear. Fear sometimes confuses Christians, but it shouldn't. Fear is a natural emotion, but having God on your side will help to propel you forward despite the fear. The easiest way to combat fear is simply to whisper a prayer to set your mind on God so you can carry on.

Goliath was over ten-and-a-half feet tall, with an entire army at his back. Don't you think David was fearful? He was probably terrified. But God was with David, and the young man moved forward despite the fear. David was working while everyone else was worrying.

David had filled his bag not just with rocks but also with prayer. When you move forward in faith, make sure that your bag is packed full of prayers. David had spent serious time in fervent prayer. His time with God ensured that when he was marching on Goliath, he gave the name of the Lord instead of his own. Pray mightily before attempting battle.

How can a tiny rock take down a giant? If we let Him, God works in ways we could never imagine. God helped to direct that rock to the weak point on Goliath's head. David had to have faith, to pray, and to move forward toward the danger, but the battle was the Lord's. No one would have guessed the outcome, but that's the kind of God we serve.

As you look at the frame you're building, know that God is shaping you and calling you to something specific. Who would have guessed that God had far more for David that would shape him into one of the most prolific Bible writers, as well as a king who founded an entire dynasty? God did.

God will tell you what to do in His time. Your job is to move forward with a champion mindset, obeying Him so that He can bless and direct you. Your God-based frame will help to make you the champion God has called you to be.

WORKBOOK

Chapter Four Questions

Question: Why are Christians champions? What is the nature of the battle a Christian faces? Who is the enemy?

_____

_____

_____

_____

_____

_____

_____

_____

_____

_____

_____

Question: Champions don't give up. What are some things that can keep you from giving up when facing overwhelming challenges?

_____
_____
_____
_____
_____
_____
_____
_____
_____
_____

Question: How should a champion respond to feelings of fear? Describe a time when prayer gave you courage and helped you to stay focused.

_____
_____
_____
_____
_____
_____

_____

_____

_____

_____

_____

Action: Write out a list of trash talk or threats that Satan tries to use against you. Next to each lie, write a statement of truth and at least one Bible verse on which it is based.

Chapter Four Notes

CHAPTER FIVE

The Seven P's, Factor #4: Prioritizing— What Are You Doing?

Actions speak louder than words, but what actions are you choosing?

That's a lesson Glenn Robinson III, winner of the 2017 NBA Slam Dunk Contest, learned from his grandmother.

As a high schooler, all he wanted to do was dunk a basketball. It's what the fans wanted, and frankly, it was the best part of the game. As a freshman, he tried everything he could do to jump high enough so that he could reach the rim, but nothing he did stretched him tall enough to dunk the ball.

One day, he admitted his troubles to his grandmother. She placed her hands on her hips and sternly said, "You need to stop trying to dunk and focus on shooting."[4]

Robinson reluctantly listened, positive that his grandmother was not the greatest authority on basketball, and he started working on his shooting. Soon he was practicing up to five hundred shots a day, working for a full year to perfect his jump shot.

He stopped thinking of dunking, and the rest of his

game improved. During his sophomore year, he found himself on a fast break, charging down the court. In his excitement, he jumped for the layup with everything he had, and he found himself not just touching the rim, but going far over. He slammed the ball through the hoop. It was then that he realized his grandmother knew best.

Robinson heeded wise counsel and changed his priorities, resulting in not only the slam dunk, but also a perfected jump shot, an improved game overall, and an NBA career.

Prioritizing goals is not just important for athletes. It will help us, as Christians, to build a godly frame for life.

Does God Like What I'm Doing?

Why do you call me "Lord, Lord," and not do what I tell you?
—Luke 6:46

The telephone rings. It's your mom.

"What are you doing?" she asks.

It's a natural question. We want a picture of what our loved ones are doing so that we can feel like we've captured a moment of their day and find out if they're doing something worthwhile.

God knows exactly what we're doing all the time. Even more, He knows why. If we make God our first priority, we will please our Lord and receive His blessing. That's why Paul wrote, "Whatever you do, work heartily, as for the Lord and not for men, knowing that from the Lord you will receive the inheritance as your reward. You are serving the Lord Christ" (Colossians 3:23–24). There's no need to obey for selfish reasons. When building your framework, doing the work for Him is the only way you're going to receive a reward.

But it's more serious than trying to get rewards; it's about truly knowing God. If we love Him, truly love Him, we'll be working for Him, not for reward. Many do good works but don't know Him.

> *Not everyone who says to me, "Lord, Lord," will enter the kingdom of heaven, but the one who does the will of my Father who is in heaven. On that day many will say to me, "Lord, Lord, did we not prophesy in your name, and cast out demons in your name, and do many mighty works in your name?" And then will I declare to them, "I never knew you; depart from me, you workers of lawlessness."*
> —**Matthew 7:21-23**

Yes, your actions speak louder than words. But your heart speaks loudest to God.

Actions and Plans in Three Parts

So, how do we make sure that our hearts are close to Him and our actions follow suit? Let's discuss a three-part plan that will help you to develop your actions into a lifestyle that reflects your faith.

Part One: Listen to Authorized Leaders

In Acts 27, Paul had been arrested for causing trouble. He was preaching Christ, and many religious Jews wanted Paul killed. In a popular trial, Paul demanded that he have his case heard before Caesar in Rome, and as a Roman citizen, Paul had that right.

So, Paul was ushered onto a boat that would take him across the Mediterranean. The voyage was doomed from the beginning. Every time they left a port, the weather grew worse and worse.

At one port, they barely made it safely to shore. Paul pulled them aside, saying, "Sirs, I perceive that the voyage will be with injury and much loss, not only of the cargo and the ship, but also of our lives" (Acts 27:9–10). But no one listened.

When a godly man or woman offers warnings about your pending actions, listen. Like Paul, who was not only wise but also filled with the Holy Spirit, Christian leaders are put into positions of authority for a reason. They have wisdom and experiences, and we should listen to them so that our actions might reflect wisdom and godliness. Wise counsel should always be welcome.

Part Two: Correct Actions Lead to Correct Reactions

The men on the ship didn't listen to Paul. As they sailed along the coast of Crete, a strong storm caught the ship, and they couldn't turn into the wind. The strong breeze carried them along. Tossed on the waves, they jettisoned cargo. They didn't see the sun or stars for days, only thick clouds. They lost all hope.

> *Since they had been without food for a long time, Paul stood up among them and said, "Men, you should have listened to me and not have set sail from Crete and incurred this injury and loss. Yet now I urge you to take heart, for there will be no loss of life among you, but only of the ship. For this very night there stood before me an angel of the God to whom I belong and whom I worship, and he said, 'Do not be afraid, Paul; you must stand before Caesar. And behold, God has granted you all those who sail with you.' So take heart, men, for I have faith in God that it will be exactly as I have been told. But we must run aground on some island."*
>
> *—Acts 27:21–26*

It's never too late to readjust your actions. Even if you didn't listen the first time, you can still steer your actions toward God's will. That doesn't mean you'll skip the consequences, and it doesn't mean you'll still receive God's full blessing, but you'll be traveling back under His direction.

Part Three: Take Heart in God's Word

The men on the ship listened, and they eventually ran safely aground. The people on the island were kind and cared for them, and the natives were able to witness the power of God's miracles, as we learn in Acts 28. Paul used his actions and his heart for God to display compassion for his shipmates and jailers.

Are you a mature Christian like Paul? Do you teach the younger, newer Christians? They must learn what the Christian life looks like through positive reinforcement and solid biblical teaching. But there's more. Paul didn't just use his wisdom and experiences to share with Christians; he also shared with unbelievers.

There are many examples in Paul's life, but we see in the example from Acts 28 how Paul's anointed framework provided him with a balanced knowledge of the sea and the Savior to allow him to reach both the sailors and the islanders. Your framework must have balanced knowledge.

When Your Actions Are Wrong

When we're doing wrong, God gets our attention in many ways. It could be conviction from reading our Bibles and praying, a sermon, or wise counsel from a trusted mentor. Sometimes God even closes doors as we walk down a path, making an end to an opportunity. Sometimes the situation will be so miserable that we turn back to God, no matter how far we've run away from Him.

As you continually build and review your frame, keep looking to God to direct your actions. Like Glenn Robinson III, you may find yourself doing far more than you ever dreamed.

WORKBOOK

Chapter Five Questions

Question: How would your habits and daily routine change if you were constantly conscious of the reality that God knows exactly what you are doing?

_____
_____
_____
_____
_____
_____
_____
_____
_____
_____
_____

Question: Do you listen to warnings and wise counsel from godly mentors and leaders? Describe a time when you did or did not listen and the results you experienced.

_____
_____
_____
_____
_____
_____
_____
_____
_____
_____

Question: What are some ways God gets our attention when we are off course? Is it ever too late to repent and change direction? Why or why not?

_____
_____
_____
_____
_____
_____

_____

_____

_____

_____

_____

Action: Like Paul, what wisdom can you share with newer Christians or unbelievers? Make a list of your most profound life experiences and the lessons God has taught you through them. How and with whom could you share a personal life lesson this week?

Chapter Five Notes

CHAPTER SIX

The Seven P's, Factor #5: Patient— Send Your Worries to God

A newly retired couple hoped to sell their house, move across the country, and live near one of their daughters. However, there were obstacles in the way. The wife worried about how things could possibly work.

She told herself that she was trying to plan for the future. She drew up countless lists in a journal as well as activity charts for everyone, and she detailed by the hour how the sale, move, and new house would proceed.

When the time came, the housing market in their home town shot up so high that the couple was stunned. They sold their house for far more than they'd ever imagined. The housing market where their daughter lived, however, was competitive. The wife checked her lists and charts, and even though they had extra money from the sale, she did not know how they were ever going to find a place to live. There was no room on her charts for something like this. She chucked aside the journal, frustrated.

Miraculously, the couple found a fantastic house whose renters wanted to stay a few more months, enabling them to continue with the sale of their house back east and the move. Busy with getting everything arranged, the wife soon forgot about her lists and plans, until later, as they unpacked, she came across the journal with her plans. She thumbed through it. Nothing had worked as she'd planned. It had worked out better, far better.

She kept the journal because she couldn't believe how God had worked things out. Despite her worrying, all had gone wonderfully. If she'd forced her plan, the move wouldn't have gone so well.

While planning is necessary, this woman had surpassed jotting down a list of to-dos. She was actually trying to control God's will for her life.

> *Therefore do not be anxious about tomorrow, for tomorrow will be anxious for itself. Sufficient for the day is its own trouble.*
> **—Matthew 6:34**

We often spend so much time fretting about what will come that we stop trusting in God's provision. When the moment we've worried about comes, it breezes by, and all we've done is waste time and create unnecessary anxiety. Worry doesn't take the sorrow out of tomorrow; it takes the strength away from today. When you arrive at tomorrow after a period of heavy worry, you're out of strength from the overload. Church is a fantastic place to release all your worries to God, frame your mind, and receive peace.

Many of us are trying to be spiritual superheroes, thinking, "I can handle this." No, you can't! A commonly held belief is encompassed in the saying "God won't give you more than you can bear." That's not in the Bible. The Bible does provide a promise that God will always be with you, helping you through whatever you have to bear.

Psalm 68:19 says, "Blessed be the Lord, who daily bears us up; God is our salvation." Jesus promised, "Come to me, all who labor and are heavy laden, and I will give you rest" (Matthew 11:28).

First Corinthians 10:13 says, "God is faithful, and he will not let you be tempted beyond your ability, but with the temptation he will also provide the way of escape, that you may be able to endure it." This passage specifically points to temptations, and it offers the reassurance that there is *always* a way not to sin—thank God!

Worry and the Last Loaf of Bread

An Israelite widow was gathering sticks by the gate (1 Kings 17). There was no doubt this would be the last time she would need fuel. There was but one small pinch of flour and a drop of oil to make a morsel for her and her son. After that, there was no more, not even to be bought. Israel's drought had killed the crops and sucked up the water. She held close to her the few dead sticks she could find.

A man sat by the city gate. He called out to her, "Bring me a little water in a vessel, that I may drink" (1 Kings 17:10).

She went to do as the man asked, but he added, "Bring me a morsel of bread in your hand" (1 Kings 17:11).

The woman replied, "As the LORD your God lives, I have nothing baked, only a handful of flour in a jar and a little oil in a jug. And now I am gathering a couple of sticks that I may go in and prepare it for myself and my son, that we may eat it and die" (1 Kings 17:12). Her voice wavered as she spoke.

What she said was true. Her worry was palpable. Death was common in that day, with little or no government to help.

Read what happened next:

> *And Elijah said to her, "Do not fear; go and do as you have said. But first make me a little cake of it and bring it to me, and afterward make something for yourself and your son. For thus says the LORD, the God of Israel, 'The jar of flour shall not be spent, and the jug of oil shall not be empty, until the day that the LORD sends rain upon the earth.'"*
> *—1 Kings 17:13-14*

The woman did as Elijah said, and everything she was promised came to pass. Trust God. He will provide even more than you hope for, think, or imagine (Ephesians 3:20). Offer up your worries in prayer!

It appeared that the widow's troubles were over, right? We wish that God allowed only one bit of trouble, just to test us and help us grow. If only life worked that way. For this woman, trouble hit again soon after:

> *After this the son of the woman, the mistress of the house, became ill. And his illness was so severe that there was no breath left in him. And she said to Elijah, "What have you against me, O man of God? You have come to me to bring my sin to remembrance and to cause the death of my son!"*
> *—1 Kings 17:17-18*

Elijah provided food and water. But the death of the woman's son hit hard, and she blamed Elijah. Even though her son was going to die anyway, the boy's death made the food seem like a small issue.

If you trust God in the little things, He will bless you in the big things. First, she had to trust Him over a little bit of bread. God was saying, "If you trust Me over this little thing, then trust Me over this big thing. I will raise your son from the dead."

> *And he said to her, "Give me your son." And he took him from her arms and carried him up into the upper chamber where he lodged, and laid him on his own bed. And he cried to the LORD, "O LORD my God, have you brought calamity even upon the widow with whom I sojourn, by killing her son?" Then he stretched himself upon the child three times and cried to the LORD, "O LORD my God, let this child's life come into him again." And the LORD listened to the voice of Elijah. And the life of the child came into him again, and he revived. And Elijah took the child and brought him down from the upper chamber into the house and delivered him to his mother. And Elijah said, "See, your son lives." And the woman said to Elijah, "Now I know that you are a man of God, and that the word of the LORD in your mouth is truth."*
> —*1 Kings 17:19-24*

What were the final words from the woman? What lesson did she learn from all of her trials? She learned to trust Elijah as a man of God, and she learned that Elijah spoke truth. When things went bad, she took the problems out of God's hands and added them into her life. She just needed to give them back to God.

If you trust in the Lord and do what He says, He will bring life back into your body. Like a rejuvenation of purpose, the boy came back to life. You can have that rejuvenation, as well. Give your worries to God.

There's no way to know exactly what God has planned for each of us. Sometimes His plans are difficult. After all, His plan for His own Son was that Jesus would be beaten and killed. However, look at the eternal consequences of Jesus' obedience!

Almost all the disciples were martyred for their faith, but they knew that declaring Jesus as Lord was worth the sacrifice. They had learned that giving up their temporary lives for eternity with Christ was worthwhile (2 Corinthians 4:17–18).

Fear often holds us back from building a strong frame

for our lives. What do you fear? What worries you about the future? Read the Word. So many examples, so many lessons, and so many promises from God are clearly described. The Bible builds us up, while worry tears us down.

When worry hits, read the Bible and pray. Imagine yourself handing your worries to God each and every time they start to plague you. Put your worries in God's inbox and rest in the assurance that He will take care of you in the small things and the big. He will sustain your frame when the winds of worry blow.

WORKBOOK

Chapter Six Questions

Question: What is the difference between planning and worrying?

_____
_____
_____
_____
_____
_____
_____
_____
_____
_____
_____

Question: What are some of the consequences for worry, both generally and in your own life?

_____
_____
_____
_____
_____
_____
_____
_____
_____
_____

Question: What are some ways to combat worry? Does trusting the Lord mean that nothing bad will ever happen? How can you trust God while knowing that He may allow deep suffering in your life?

_____
_____
_____
_____
_____

_____

_____

_____

_____

_____

Action: Make a list of your fears and worries. Beside each, write a scripture that provides hope or comfort. Then offer up the list to God in prayer. Imagine yourself handing Him each worry, one at a time, until they're gone.

Chapter Six Notes

CHAPTER SEVEN

The Seven P's, Factor #6: Productive— Doing the Most

Mother Teresa was a young nun teaching in India when she felt God calling her to leave teaching and move to the slums of Calcutta to care for the poor.[5] However, it took a year and a half for her to get permission to follow through with her dream. When the okay was finally given, she was offered very basic medical training, and then she moved to Calcutta with the goal of caring for the neglected poor.

With this very humble goal, she eventually impacted thousands of untouchable people and became the poster woman for giving and caring. Even though she dedicated her life to Christ when she became a nun, she wasn't doing the most she could do until she answered God's call to serve the poor, her true calling.

Mother Teresa had built a powerful connection with God before moving into her calling. Her framework was built on the Word, and then she worked from within the frame.

Most of us aren't Mother Teresa. When it comes to our Christian faith, we are often much better at talking the most and doing the least. We know the Christian language. We know the Christian dance. We can look like good Christians when we are around other Christians, which is usually once a week. We talk a really good game about our faith. We rely on the Christian mindset of faith in God that somehow, someway, He will make good things happen.

Let's not just talk. Let's be about God's work. Doing the most means working right from the center of our framework. Let me say it again: doing the most. *Doing* means actively working. *The most* means more and more until we're functioning at our peak capacity.

> *Finally, then, brothers, we ask and urge you in the Lord Jesus, that as you received from us how you ought to walk and to please God, just as you are doing, that you do so more and more. For you know what instructions we gave you through the Lord Jesus.*
> —*1 Thessalonians 4:1–2*

The Thessalonian church had built an amazing framework, which gave Paul opportunity to make such a statement. What if you were to receive a text message from God that read, "You're currently pleasing Me, but do so more and more." Where you are is not your finishing line, so don't stall out. You need to increase your actions until you are doing the most!

Pleasing People

Does doing more simply mean pleasing more people? It's easy to fall into the habit of pleasing people instead of God. Unfortunately, pleasing others is a bottomless pit that we can never fill up. Many people want more and more. On the other hand, working to please God quickly overflows and pours out onto everyone around us. Pleasing God is a win-win for everyone in the long-term.

Do you remember the story of Noah that begins in Genesis 6? He was old and living in a world filled with sin when God called on him to build a framework large enough to hold his family and two of almost every animal to protect them during an impending flood. It had never rained before, yet as the gopher-wood planks took shape, Noah kept working even when he was mocked. He didn't want to please people. He wanted to please God, and it ultimately saved his family from destruction.

As with Noah, it's not our responsibility to be concerned about what other people think of us. They may speak well of us; they may speak ill of us. They may ignore us altogether. It doesn't matter. We are to listen to only one voice, that of our Good Shepherd. Jesus said, "My sheep hear my voice, and I know them, and they follow me. I give them eternal life, and they will never perish, and no one will snatch them out of my hand" (John 10:27–28).

God designed our framework for His own pleasure. Pleasing people usually produces immediate and positive results with some adverse long-term consequences. On the other hand, pleasing God produces results that aren't always instantaneous but impact His greater plan for the good. It's like the choice between eating a massive sundae with bananas, chocolate, nuts, and whipped cream or skipping it to eat something healthy. The sundae gives us instant gratification, but the effects to the waistline are long-term, with even worse potential health problems like diabetes. Choosing healthier options isn't easy, but you know it's what's best for you.

Please God first, and then you will better know how to serve others. You're not just making others happy. You are pleasing God and loving those around you, and God will reward you.

How do you know that God will reward you? How do you know that pleasing people isn't the answer and that pleasing God will result in the long-term best? We know because of the witness of Scripture, the witness of the church through history, and the witness of other believers around us. Their stories of faith remind us that pleasing God always turns out to be the best framework.

Faith

> *And without faith it is impossible to please him, for whoever would draw near to God must believe that he exists and that he rewards those who seek him.*
> *—Hebrews 11:6*

If you are going to do the most, then do the most to please God. Remember, a reward is coming. When we do the most to please other people, what is our reward—that they're happy with us? Truly, compared to the gifts we receive from God, people give us nothing. If you don't keep pleasing people, they will eventually cut you off. Please God first and let the "people chips" fall where they may.

You need to love people, but love Jesus first. Loving Jesus first means doing as He asks. Sometimes Jesus asks you to wash someone else's dishes. Sometimes He asks you to teach that person to wash his own dishes. Sometimes He asks you to let the person figure it out on his own, in hopes that he will be so frustrated with the dishes that he will turn to Jesus. It's a silly example but one that can be applied to life for a strong framework. So, how do we combine pleasing God, faith, and doing the most?

Begin with prayer. Ask God to help you build a life that pleases Him. Prayer is simply talking to God, making your requests known, thanking Him for helping to build the framework of your life, and telling Him that you trust Him with the future. Prayer is the foundation of your frame.

Read your Bible. God loves it when we spend time with Him. Is there a time in your day when you can set aside five minutes to be with Him? Start building that habit by implementing a daily Bible reading time. Then stretch it to ten minutes when you're ready. The Word of God is the proof of His character. If we feel uneasy about our faith in Him, we're not going to do our best, nor are we going to sell out completely for Him. The Bible will calm our fears and show us that He is faithful to fulfill His promises. The Scriptures are the nails that hold our frame together.

Spend time thanking God and praising Him for who He is. Do this all day with little things. Did you lose your car keys and then find them right away? Thank God! Did you get a small bonus at work? Wow, that's something to thank God about! If someone praises you, thank the person and thank God. This is the best way to build a strong foundational framework.

Do the right thing, no matter the circumstance. Hebrews 13:16 says, "Do not neglect to do good and to share what you have, for such sacrifices are pleasing to God." No matter what we're going through, in times of little and times of plenty, we always have the choice to do good and to give of ourselves.

Love God's people. Remember, you're not pleasing other people; you're loving them. Psalm 149:4 says, "For the LORD takes pleasure in his people; he adorns the humble with salvation." Humility means that you are going to do all you can as directed by God to make sure that things are in order.

Do your most from a good framework, combined with your faith in God, and He will reward you.

WORKBOOK

Chapter Seven Questions

Question: Think of a Christian you know who spends more time doing than talking about what should be done. What does this person's actions indicate about his or her faith? Which characterizes your life, more talking or more doing?

_____
_____
_____
_____
_____
_____
_____
_____
_____
_____
_____

Question: Why is people-pleasing a trap? How can you avoid it? What is the difference between loving people and pleasing them? Describe a time when truly loving a person may require displeasing him or her.

_____
_____
_____
_____
_____
_____
_____
_____
_____
_____

Question: What are some attitudes and actions that please God? How can you grow in each of these?

_____
_____
_____
_____
_____
_____
_____

_____

_____

_____

_____

_____

Action: Ask a trusted Christian friend to help you determine ways that you can do more and to keep you accountable to doing more. Remember, the goal is not to be busier or merely to add activities, but to increase in fulfilling God's call on your life.

Chapter Seven Notes

CHAPTER EIGHT

The Seven P's, Factor #7: Professional— Independent from Outside Control

The British Empire in the late 1700s was arguably the most powerful in the world. With the help of numerous colonies importing goods, Great Britain's tax base was strong, and they built a powerful army to back up their strength when collecting taxes.

The thirteen colonies in America were getting unruly, and they wanted to break ties with Britain. Keeping the French from taking land in America had cost the British quite a bit of money, and as a result, the British taxed the colonies so heavily that many of the Acts were technically illegal.

At last, the colonists had enough. The tax abuse had depleted their will to comply. In 1776, representatives of the thirteen colonies came together to write one of the most powerful documents in history:

> When in the Course of human events, it becomes necessary for one people to dissolve the political bands which have connected them with another, and to assume among the powers of the earth, the separate and equal station to which the Laws of Nature and of Nature's God entitle them, a decent respect to the opinions of mankind requires that they should declare the causes which impel them to the separation.
>
> We hold these truths to be self-evident, that all men are created equal, that they are endowed by their Creator with certain unalienable Rights, that among these are Life, Liberty and the pursuit of Happiness. —That to secure these rights, Governments are instituted among Men, deriving their just powers from the consent of the governed, —That whenever any Form of Government becomes destructive of these ends, it is the Right of the People to alter or to abolish it, and to institute new Government, laying its foundation on such principles and organizing its powers in such form, as to them shall seem most likely to effect their Safety and Happiness.
> —**The Declaration of Independence**
> **In Congress, July 4, 1776**

In that moment, an idea was planted, and the war for America's independence began. The decision didn't happen overnight. For years, the greatest thinkers in America debated, the people rallied, and God led them to freedom. Supporters created long lists of reasons to break from England almost daily prior to the war and during the fight.

As Christians, we can make a long list of reasons to break from Satan. Our independence from sin, like America's independence from England, doesn't just happen on its own. The break is carefully framed through deep thought and intense purpose, all directed by God. A statement within the Declaration of Independence speaks about the foundation needed to institute a new government. A strong, well-established foundational framework ensures freedom and future success.

We're not talking about worldly freedom here, but rather freedom from evil, from sin, and from the devil. We're talking about an eternal freedom.

Breaking from the Bondage of Sin

Live as people who are free, not using your freedom as a cover-up for evil, but living as servants of God.
—*1 Peter 2:16*

We aren't meant to live as slaves in bondage to the things of this world. It's time to declare your independence from sin!

The Declaration of Independence makes this claim:

> We hold these truths to be self-evident, that all men are created equal, that they are endowed by their Creator with certain unalienable Rights, that among these are Life, Liberty and the pursuit of Happiness.

You can't have life, liberty, or happiness if you are controlled by outside forces. We want to move from worldly sin to spiritual freedom.

Your spiritual framework has qualified you as a professional Christian. A professional is someone who has obtained qualifications and become occupationally proficient or even an expert, often resulting in superior earnings. Your status as a professional Christian enables you to bear an increased yield of spiritual fruit. However, Romans 6:22 gives us a warning: "But now that you have been set free from sin and have become slaves of God, the fruit you get leads to sanctification and its end, eternal life."

We use our freedom poorly when we choose to be

dependent on things other than God. We see things as good, but over time, they take hold of us and prevent us from experiencing God's best for our lives.

Even small things in our lives can be sinful if we let them: gossiping about someone, looking at someone perversely, indulging in sinful actions. It's better to run away when temptation comes knocking than to fall victim to the enemy's plans.

Independence from sin allows you to preach the gospel. If the Spirit is upon you, then you are free, and the devil can't hold you back. You have been set free to help free others. Independence from your sin allows you to preach the gospel effectively.

Can't Break Free?

It's one thing to know that you should break free from sin, as we've discussed, but it's quite another thing to declare your independence. Begin by asking the Holy Spirit to help you see what is holding you prisoner. What habits, relationships, and sins are keeping you from doing what God wants you to be doing?

You don't have to fix everything all at once. Choose one thing you can do to step toward freedom. Maybe it's buying healthier food. It might be that you stop watching a particular TV show or listening to certain music. Perhaps you shouldn't spend time with someone who tends to lead you down the wrong path.

Write your goals in your journal or on a card and place it somewhere you will see it daily. Ask God to help you meet your goals.

Now is the time to declare independence from sin. Just as America broke free from Great Britain and established its independent framework, you can break free from sinful bondage and establish your anointed, independent frame work. Then you will be equipped to help others do the same.

WORKBOOK

Chapter Eight Questions

Question: What is the connection between sin and bondage? What sin have you allowed into your life only to find yourself enslaved to it later?

_____

_____

_____

_____

_____

_____

_____

_____

_____

_____

_____

Question: What are some specific things that lead you into temptation but might not affect others in the same way? Why is it important not to judge others who have stricter or less strict standards? Look at the principles of Christian liberty found in Romans 14.

_____

_____

_____

_____

_____

_____

_____

_____

_____

_____

Question: How and in what ways does your ministry potential increase when you break free from the strongholds of sin?

_____

_____

_____

_____

_____

_____

_____

_____

_____

_____

_____

Action: Write your spiritual declaration of independence, declaring your freedom from Satan and the specific sins that have bound you. Incorporate helpful scriptures, such as those found in Romans 6–8, into your declaration. Put it where you will see it often. What is a practical next step you can take toward your freedom?

Chapter Eight Notes

CHAPTER NINE

Don't Even Think About It

Finally, brothers, whatever is true, whatever is honorable, whatever is just, whatever is pure, whatever is lovely, whatever is commendable, if there is any excellence, if there is anything worthy of praise, think about these things.
—***Philippians 4:8***

The Bible is clear that Christians are to keep their minds pure and holy.

This reminds me of a story about a wealthy father who pampered his young son. As the teenager approached his high school graduation, he saw a beautiful sports car in a showroom and wanted his father to buy it as a graduation present. The day he saw that car in the showroom, he began giving certain signs to his father that he wanted the car.

The young man was excited. Surely his father would purchase the car. He always got whatever he wanted from his dad.

Finally, graduation day came. His father called him into his study and asked him to sit. He brought in a beautifully wrapped gift, expressing how proud he was of his son for reaching this rite of passage.

The young man ripped open the box, hoping to see a key to the sports car inside, but what he found instead was a book. Angry, he raised his voice and said to his father, "With all your money, you got me *this*?"

The boy stormed out of the house, leaving the book behind. His father called out, but the boy refused to come back.

The two remained estranged for many years. The young man became a successful businessman, just like his father. He hadn't seen his father since graduation day, and he wasn't sure he missed him at all. Most of the time, he didn't even think of his father.

One day, he received a telegram saying that his father had passed away. He had willed all his possessions to his son, and the son needed to come and take care of things left behind by his father.

When he arrived at his father's house, sadness and regret filled his heart. He went to the study, where he had last spoken with his father. He began to sort through his father's drawers and, surprisingly, found the same book his father had given him on his graduation day. The memories came back in a flash. He sat down in the same chair, and, with tears rolling down his face, he opened the book and turned the pages.

After reaching the middle of the book, he found a hole inside of it with a car key and a tag. On the tag was written: *With love for my precious son, who has made me so proud.*

Thinking Our Best

Many times in life, we make snap judgments about people and experiences because they don't meet our predefined expectations. Unfortunately, these drastic choices create long-term misunderstandings and conflicts. If only we would think positively when tempted to judge based on our first impression! Misunderstanding can often be prevented by practicing what I like to call *nonjudgmental inquisitive communication*. In other words, ask the person questions instead of assuming dishonorable intentions.

In times of anger, we need to stop for a moment and think before making any harsh judgments about a person or a situation. The person may have not wronged us at all. If we have been wronged, we need to learn to forgive before it's too late.

We are often our own greatest stumbling block when it comes to framing our lives in a godly way. The human mind can lead us to commit heinous acts and crimes. You may say, "I am not in jail. I don't have a record." Not in the natural, worldly sense, but in the spiritual realm, many of us continue to be offenders. Don't allow your mind into dark places. A sound framework has numerous windows for spiritual light!

How to Elevate Your Thinking

Developing Christlike thinking will help us build a stronger framework. How do we fix our thoughts?

Spend time in the Scriptures. Let God's words change your thoughts.

Count your blessings. Instead of thinking about temporary problems, concentrate on what you are grateful for. The adversary wants you to focus on living a gloomy and frustrated life instead of focusing on the blessings of life, with Jesus leading the way.

Allow joy into your heart. Gratitude from counting your blessings leads to joy. Don't undermine joy by returning to your problems. Jesus wants us to be joyful. We need to keep our eyes on Jesus when things get difficult. Philippians 1:25 is one of many verses that talk about joy: "Convinced of this, I know that I will remain and continue with you all, for your progress and joy in the faith...."

Turn away from worrying thoughts. Why worry yourself to death by replaying bad memories over and over? Stop playing negative reruns in your mind. So what if you said the wrong thing? Did you seek and receive forgiveness? Let it go! Do you have something major causing you worry? Give it to God, minute by minute, hour by hour, day by day.

Carefully control your emotions. Emotions are temporary and ever-changing, and they often betray us. Know that annoyance and frustration are problems we need to deal with ourselves. You can only control your reaction to other people's actions, not their actions.

Christians sometimes are the most stern, stagnated, and hard people. Learn to be happy and joyful instead. You will live longer!

Avoiding Mind Traps

And the woman said to the serpent, "We may eat of the fruit of the trees in the garden...."
—Genesis 3:2

Eve was engaged in a conversation with the devil, one she was not equipped to win. He twisted and masked his words to get her off focus. The devil told a half-truth. A half-truth is a whole lie. And Eve listened to the devil:

So when the woman saw that the tree was good for food, and that it was a delight to the eyes, and that the tree was to be desired to make one wise, she took of its fruit and ate, and she also gave some to her husband who was with her, and he ate.
—Genesis 3:6

Eve was easily convinced that God was keeping something great from her. Her thoughts made her vulnerable. God gave Adam and Eve simple directions not to eat from a certain tree. The issue was not about access; it was about accountability.

God has given us unlimited access to wisdom through His Holy Spirit and His Word, which guide us and guard our thought processes. It is extremely important to be aware of what's going into your mind. If your framework is not spiritually protected by the Spirit and the Word, ungodly things may seep into your thoughts and result in dangerous consequences.

Eve simply should not have engaged in a conversation with the serpent. If something doesn't sit right when someone is trying to talk you into something, if it feels *iffy*, tell yourself, "Don't even think about it." Then turn and walk away. They aren't trying to deal with the verbiage, articulation, and interpretation of what the Bible says. They are trying to get at your soul. Stay aware and vigilantly protect your mind.

WORKBOOK

Chapter Nine Questions

Question: Describe a time when you assumed the worst about a person or situation only to find out the truth later. What impact did your quick judgment have on your relationship with that person?

_____

_____

_____

_____

_____

_____

_____

_____

_____

_____

_____

Question: Do you actively seek to own and control your thoughts, or do you let them have free reign? What are some practical ways you can "take every thought captive to obey Christ" (2 Corinthians 10:5)?

_____
_____
_____
_____
_____
_____
_____
_____
_____

Question: Describe the mind traps that Satan sets. Why are these so dangerous and powerful? How can you avoid them?

_____
_____
_____
_____
_____

_____

_____

_____

_____

_____

Action: Read Matthew 4. Why was Jesus physically vulnerable? How did Jesus overcome Satan's mind traps? What can you learn from His strategy, and how will you implement it?

Chapter Nine Notes

CHAPTER TEN

Wrong Place, Right Praise

> *Let everything that has breath praise the LORD! Praise the LORD!*
> —***Psalm 150:6***

As Paul and Silas, brothers in Christ, were traveling to the city gate in Philippi for a time of prayer with other believers, they were met by a slave girl who was a fortune teller with a demonic spirit inside of her:

> *She followed Paul and us, crying out, "These men are servants of the Most High God, who proclaim to you the way of salvation." And this she kept doing for many days. Paul, having become greatly annoyed, turned and said to the spirit, "I command you in the name of Jesus Christ to come out of her." And it came out that very hour.*
> —***Acts 16:17-18***

The slave girl's owners were furious. Without the demonic spirit, she wouldn't be able to tell fortunes and bring them income. They brought in the magistrates and accused Paul and Silas of breaking the law. Paul and Silas were beaten and thrown into prison, where their feet were bound in stocks.

Do you think that Paul and Silas should have been furious? They delivered the poor girl from her demons, and the thanks they received was a beating and jail time. They were jailed for preaching the good news of Christ's death and resurrection. One might say that they were in the wrong place. But wait; keep reading.

Locked in a cell with the prospect of death in the very near future, they surely thought that they were in the wrong place. With little hope of escape, what do you think they did? They praised God: "About midnight Paul and Silas were praying and singing hymns to God, and the prisoners were listening to them" (Acts 16:25).

It seems like prison would be the wrong place to be praying and singing, but read what happened next:

> ...and suddenly there was a great earthquake, so that the foundations of the prison were shaken. And immediately all the doors were opened, and everyone's bonds were unfastened. When the jailer woke and saw that the prison doors were open, he drew his sword and was about to kill himself, supposing that the prisoners had escaped. But Paul cried with a loud voice, "Do not harm yourself, for we are all here." And the jailer called for lights and rushed in, and trembling with fear he fell down before Paul and Silas. Then he brought them out and said, "Sirs, what must I do to be saved?" And they said, "Believe in the Lord Jesus, and you will be saved, you and your household." And they spoke the word of the Lord to him and to all who were in his house. And he took them the same hour of the night and washed their wounds; and he was baptized at once, he and all his family.
>
> —*Acts 16:26-33*

Overcoming the Wrong Place

As you build your life framework, more often than not, there will be people who become upset with you. Why? Because they stopped building their framework and don't want to be shown up. You may experience people trying to tear down your framework. Be prepared for the devil to follow you and attempt to introduce doubt about God's work in your life as you do ministry, pray, or serve others. Nevertheless, in the midst of it, other people will see the truth of who you are.

You become a target for Satan as your framework becomes stronger. Sometimes the devil will do things to try to imprison you. You think that you're doing what God wants, yet the stocks clamp in place over your legs, the door of your cell closes, and it feels as if there's no hope. You've tried to do what God has called you to do, but you still end up in the wrong place. What do you do?

Praise God! Sing! Worship Him!

People are listening. Paul and Silas started singing, and the Bible says that the prisoners were listening. Their worship changed lives. When you praise God, people will listen. Not only will others listen, but the devil will start listening as well.

When difficulties strike, however, praising God is usually the last thing we want to do.

Check Your Attitude at the Door

Paul and Silas did God's work by freeing the slave girl from her demon. However, they had no idea that being placed in jail would offer a greater freeing work. They did not know that they would reach people with the gospel, but they proceeded to worship God and act in obedience despite their predicament.

We tend to get bent out of shape whenever anything

doesn't go our way. We want life to be easy and comfortable, and when it's not, we often blame God. When things go wrong, our tendency is to get angry, to complain, to worry, or to find some form of escape. But that's not what God wants us to do.

When Paul and Silas were in prison, they chose to praise God anyway. Even though they faced flogging and the possibility of death, they praised God. They knew that God had a good reason for putting them in such a difficult situation. They were glad to give up their comfort and freedom for the gospel.

Did Paul and Silas know that if they started praising and singing, they would find freedom? No. They knew only that God was worthy of praise, no matter their circumstances. They knew that it was a privilege to suffer for the name of the Lord Jesus.

You might find yourself behind figurative locked doors for doing the right thing, but God's already making sure that the door is going to be opened the next time you praise Him. You are going to be set free because of the right praise.

If God's already planned out your escape, then you must check your attitude. God does not intend to make our lives easy. He intends to use us to glorify Him. When we see how mighty He is and when we understand what Jesus did for us on the cross, our only reaction should be to praise Him, regardless of our circumstances. Praising God doesn't have to happen in church or through music. Just sing to the Lord. Check that attitude so that God can work.

Praising God isn't simply singing. It's thanking Him, having a grateful heart, and humbling ourselves before Him. David turned to praising and humbling himself before God at one of his lowest moments in Psalm 51. He'd committed adultery and murder and suffered the loss of a son, but he still praised God despite his sin and grief.

When we praise Him through song, prayer, and the

reading of His Word, our hearts are changed. Praising and worshiping God is the key to opening every locked door. Make sure that your framework has a praiseworthy foundation. Praise opens doors. Praise God!

WORKBOOK

Chapter Ten Questions

Question: Describe a time when you were trying to do the right thing yet ended up in a bad situation because of it. What was your natural response to this unfair suffering?

_____
_____
_____
_____
_____
_____
_____
_____
_____
_____
_____
_____

Question: Why is it hard to praise God in the midst of suffering? What are some of the potential results when you do? Is it okay to praise God even when your heart is not in it? Why or why not?

_____

_____

_____

_____

_____

_____

_____

_____

_____

_____

Question: What are some practical ways to praise God? How can you connect with Him when you are suffering physically or emotionally?

_____

_____

_____

_____

_____

_____

_____

_____

_____

_____

_____

_____

Action: Make a list of God's names. (You can ask your pastor for a recommendation of one of the many excellent resources available to aid you in this.) Which name encourages you today? How can God's names give you hope?

Action: Write an action-provoking letter to God that refers to the locations where you normally go during the week and your normal praise locations and identifies the correlation (or lack thereof) between the two sets of places.

Action: What are God's attributes, as you understand Him based on Scripture? What are your attributes?
- First, create a list of attributes to answer each question.
- Second, compare the two lists of attributes. What are the differences? Are there any similarities?
- Third, create a daily reading plan for the Psalms. After each daily reading, add any new attributes to your lists (especially God's attributes).
- Finally, list some past situations that created unusual difficulties in your life. How did certain attributes from your list hinder you in each difficult situation? How might certain godly attributes

help you through a similar situation in the future?

Chapter Ten Notes

CHAPTER ELEVEN

Frustrated but Free

A 2014 Pew Research survey[6] of 35,000 American adults showed the percentage of the population who call themselves Christians falling to 70.6%, compared to a similar 2007 survey, in which 78.4% of adults identified as Christians. People who didn't affiliate with any faith, sometimes known as *nones* for choosing "none of the above," represented 22.8% of American adults in 2014, according to the Pew study. In comparison, evangelical Protestants made up 25.4%, Catholics made up 20.8%, and mainline Protestants represented 14.7%.

In the 2007 Pew survey, the unaffiliated group was 16.1% of the population, evangelical Protestants were 26.3%, mainline Protestants were 18.1%, and Catholics were 23.9%.

The Frustrated Christian

Why are so many giving up on the faith? When we, as Christians, don't live for God, we often get frustrated and quit, although we are really free in Christ.

"Frustrated but free" sounds like an oxymoron. If you are frustrated, how can you really be free? I have learned and observed that many in the body of Christ claim freedom yet are still frustrated. Everyone is frustrated by something, but the manner in which some deal with frustration leads them to become even more frustrated, creating an internal prison of unhappiness, with no freedom in sight. They then leave the church because of their anguish.

> *Be not quick in your spirit to become angry, for anger lodges in the heart of fools.*
> *—Ecclesiastes 7:9*

Unresolved anger leads to frustration. Sometimes the process is nearly instantaneous. At other times, the frustration grows over time. Regardless of the process, frustration seems to work in tandem with the four following issues.

Losing Focus

As you build your framework, the adversary wants you to lose focus so that you will grow frustrated. When you lose focus, you become disoriented. Have you ever gone to the optometrist and had your eyes dilated? Losing your focus compares to having your eyes dilated. Your pupils dilate, and your vision becomes skewed. If you don't know where you are, you will end up in the wrong place. Don't let the adversary cause you to lose focus and become disoriented.

When we lose our focus, we start misinterpreting what we hear and see, causing us to lose focus even more. But when we are free from the dilating drops and can see clearly, we can refocus and head in the right direction. If you don't clear your vision and reset your focus, frustration will ensue.

Lowering Expectations

Once the adversary has your focus diverted, he can convince you to set lower expectations. Whatever has you locked down, the adversary has you looking at it instead of at your framework. That "woe is me" mindset keeps you looking at your pain and focused on your problems. But you must look past it, keep building your framework, and stay focused on Christ. Then you will start breaking free.

Levying Accusations

Some people aren't happy with their lives, so they try to drag others down with them. Frustrated people tend to frustrate other people so they can have guests in their misery. As the saying goes, "Misery loves company."

Have you ever made a rude, abrupt, or harsh statement to someone and then immediately asked yourself, "Why did I say that?" Your words can cut off future relationships and destroy your framework. Your frustration and bad days can easily turn into your refusal to show Christ's love.

By pausing before you speak, spending time in the Word, and asking God for help, you can break the cycle of transferring your frustration. Don't take your frustration out on others. Personal frustration is just that, personal. Other people should not be required to manage or correct your frustration. Instead, give your frustration to Christ and be free.

Leaving

Frustration can cause you to leave your church, your family, your friends, or your job. It can even cause you to leave the reality of who you are. But when we leave something, we often are still left with our frustrations.

When you experience frustration and want to leave your current situation, ask yourself why you are frustrated. Be honest about your reason for leaving. Are you being abused? If so, then leave. Are you involved in illegal activities? If so, then leave. If the reason for your leaving is shallow or because you're simply frustrated, it's going to cause you to run continually.

The Frustrated and the Free

If you're living a frustrated life, you're not living a free life. As you build a frustration-free framework, your life will become one of absolute freedom.

We want life to be the way we've envisioned it. However, God doesn't work that way. It takes daily mental and spiritual refocusing to remain on a peaceful track. Spending time each day reading the Bible and praying will keep you connected with God and assist with your focus.

If you have lowered your expectations of what God has in store for you, then take time to write out a gratitude journal. Add five things you're thankful for each day.

Think through who has disappointed you in your spiritual walk. Look at the issue from the other person's point of view. Were your demands reasonable? If needed, forgive this person or ask for forgiveness.

If you're considering leaving, find a spiritual mother or father and ask that person to meet with you regularly to help hold you accountable and to talk through difficult issues.

We can't please God if we are frustrated. We might be able to please other people if we are frustrated, but frustration isn't a long-term solution.

If you do right, your children and friends will be blessed. If you kick frustration out of your life, you will be free, and they will be free. They won't have to fight the demons you are fighting. If you aren't free, then your children and your family are going to become as frustrated as you are.

If you're frustrated, establish a framework logo that states: "I refuse to remain frustrated, and I demand to be free."

WORKBOOK

Chapter Eleven Questions

Question: Think about people or situations that cause you to be frustrated. What changes in your attitude need to happen for you to live out your freedom in Christ instead of remaining frustrated?

_____

_____

_____

_____

_____

_____

_____

_____

_____

_____

Question: What causes you to lose focus in your Christian life? How might you get further off track if you don't regain that focus? How can you regain it?

_____
_____
_____
_____
_____
_____
_____
_____
_____
_____

Question: *Church hopping* is a term that describes the modern phenomenon of people changing from church to church in the same geographic area, often leaving over preferences or annoyances. What are some self-centered reasons people leave their church?

_____
_____
_____
_____
_____

_____
_____
_____
_____
_____
_____
_____

Action: Make a gratitude list and thank God for all He has done. Considering how God has cared for you in the past, what should your hope and expectation be for your future?

Chapter Eleven Notes

CHAPTER TWELVE

Not Totally Correct—
But Totally Called

You were given a name right after birth, a proper name that's written on a birth certificate and documented in government records. That's the name you will be called for the rest of your life. It's on your Social Security card, it's on your driver's license, and it will be on your obituary. Your name is so important that it takes a court ruling to have it changed.

However, you may be known by a different name, a nickname. A nickname is a name that the world puts on you to describe you. It may be a fun, quirky name based on your personality.

God is calling you by a name that's documented in the records of heaven, one that cannot be changed. This name is so sacred that you should spend time daily cherishing it. The name is "child of God." You need to listen to that name and not to what everyone else is calling you. That is your eternal name. It is what you're called by the One who knows all and loves you the most. You are called by God. The name He gives you, child of God, goes on the front door of your frame forever.

> *For consider your calling, brothers: not many of you were wise according to worldly standards, not many were powerful, not many were of noble birth. But God chose what is foolish in the world to shame the wise; God chose what is weak in the world to shame the strong; God chose what is low and despised in the world, even things that are not, to bring to nothing things that are, so that no human being might boast in the presence of God.*
> —*1 Corinthians 1:26–29*

God takes your calling seriously, and so should you.

Our Mistakes Are Painful, But God Can Still Use Us

When we look at ourselves, we tend to see our mistakes and blemishes rather than the beloved children God has called us to be. Don't let mistakes stop your framework building process. Mistakes are just missed steps and actions, and you are called by God to keep going.

The twelve disciples were not scholars or gentlemen, and they weren't known for being politically correct. They were called by Jesus to be world changers. They also had nicknames, such as Sons of Thunder (Mark 3:17) and James the Younger (Mark 15:40). Mistakes and all, God loved them and used them for His glory.

Many of us want to put ourselves on trial after making a misstep. We cross-examine our frailties, call ourselves to the witness stand, and badger ourselves on the incorrectness of our actions and words. We wonder if God is ready to wash His hands of us. We think that He must be shaking His head, just hoping that we don't cause any more trouble. We start to believe that God can't or won't use us anymore, so we stop trying to move forward.

Yet, we already know that all have fallen short of God's ultimate standard, but God's gift to us is life through Christ (Romans 3:23; 6:23). God likes calling people whom the world would never choose. He walked around with tax collectors, ate meals with prostitutes, and first revealed Himself after the resurrection to women (Luke 15:2; Matthew 28:1–10), who held a very low position at the time.

The men and women who followed Jesus knew that He called them right where they were. He didn't ask for a résumé or review their pedigree. He just said, "Follow Me" (Matthew 4:19; Matthew 8:22; Matthew 9:9). From Simon and Andrew, to James and John, to the tax collector named Levi, Jesus simply said, "Follow Me."

The Calling of Levi

What caused Levi suddenly to change from fleecing his fellow Jews for all their money to leaving it all behind to follow this man named Jesus? He knew that following Jesus would cost him his livelihood, but the words that came out of Jesus' mouth were anointed with power. Levi forgot about himself and thought about God's glory. What causes a thug and bully like Levi to make this kind of change in a nanosecond? What causes a liar to make this kind of about-face instantly? It's the calling. Theologians, scientists, and historic researchers alike wonder why Jesus said these two words, "Follow Me," and people received spiritual metamorphosis in a blink of the eye. It's because He was calling each person by his real name, child of God.

> *And Levi made him a great feast in his house, and there was a large company of tax collectors and others reclining at table with them.*
> —**Luke 5:29**

Jesus knows the true name of even the most

disagreeable people. He invited the thugs and bullies to dinner first so that these types of undesirable people would invite others like them. He called you so that you will call others like yourself. People will listen to those they can relate to—that, my friend, is why your name is called!

> *And the Pharisees and their scribes grumbled at his disciples, saying, "Why do you eat and drink with tax collectors and sinners?" And Jesus answered them, "Those who are well have no need of a physician, but those who are sick."*
> **—Luke 5:30–31**

Jesus calls all of us in a continuous calling because all of us continue to do things incorrectly. We must focus on His calling. We must hear His voice and choose to follow it.

How Often Are We Forgiven for Our Mistakes?

How often will God forgive us? His standard is found in the Word:

> *Then Peter came up and said to him, "Lord, how often will my brother sin against me, and I forgive him? As many as seven times?" Jesus said to him, "I do not say to you seven times, but seventy-seven times."*
> **—Matthew 18:21–22**

Even though we all have sinful habits and have hurt people in the past, God is ready to forgive us again and again: "If we confess our sins, he is faithful and just to forgive us our sins and to cleanse us from all unrighteousness" (1 John 1:9). He also expects us to forgive continuously. You don't have to pay the price for your sins, because Jesus already paid it. Stop inflicting needless punishment on yourself for sins that God's already forgiven.

Your frame and your life are like an open book. Who is reading you today? What are you publishing in your life today? Are you focusing on the One who called you and His forgiveness? Are you listening for Him to call out your name? If you are focused on your calling, you will be focused on the answer. Jesus loves us so much that He is sitting right now at the right hand of the Father, interceding for us and calling our names (Romans 8:34).

You are forgiven! You don't need to identify yourself with your sin anymore. You must identify yourself with Christ. This is the framework you need for your life.

WORKBOOK

Chapter Twelve Questions

Question: What were some of the types of people Jesus chose to call as disciples? Why does He call so many people who seem unworthy?

_____
_____
_____
_____
_____
_____
_____
_____
_____
_____
_____
_____

Question: How and why did Jesus call normal people to be transformed? How has His calling transformed your life?

_____
_____
_____
_____
_____
_____
_____
_____
_____
_____

Question: Do you tend to accept God's forgiveness or beat yourself up over past sins and mistakes? How can you walk in your forgiveness purchased by Christ?

_____
_____
_____
_____
_____
_____

_____

_____

_____

_____

_____

Action: What name does God call you? List some names He has given to every believer (see 1 Peter 2:4–12 to get started).

Chapter Twelve Notes

CHAPTER THIRTEEN

I'm Promoted

For not from the east or from the west and not from the wilderness comes lifting up, but it is God who executes judgment, putting down one and lifting up another.
—*Psalm 75:6–7*

No matter your grade level in school, your main objective is to get promoted. Graduation is considered to be an educational requirement for success, and it signifies promotion in life.

The desire to be promoted should not stop after school. In fact, the desire for spiritual promotion should intensify. If you understand your spiritual education to be the requirement for promotion within your framework, you will guarantee lifelong success.

Promotion involves advancing, progressing, or being elevated to a higher position. When you're promoted, you're elevated to a new rank. You walk differently. You talk differently. You comb your hair a little differently. You get new school clothes. You've grown.

I've always loved academics and worked hard in school, and my promotion to the next class was always certain. Thankfully, I never had to worry about moving forward. My cousin and I were a year apart in school, and academics came a bit harder for him, unfortunately. At the end of my junior year of high school, I saw him coming down the hall, looking rather depressed. "I didn't get promoted," he said to me.

"Oh no!" I said. "Let me see your report card." When I read his report card, I saw why he didn't get promoted. There was a note at the bottom that read, "Delayed promotion, pending your attendance to summer school."

"All you have to do," I explained to him, "is finish summer school, do the time, and you will be promoted to the next grade in the fall." I put my arm around him. "You just have to put in some extra time. You might have to pay extra for summer school and a tutor. It's more than you expected, but you will be promoted."

He immediately cheered up and started walking differently. He said, "You know what, hope is not gone!"

Sometimes we may feel like we've blown it, but in fact, we've only delayed it. Hope is not lost! Press on for the promotion!

Promotion: Putting in the Work

God doesn't send us a certificate that says we're being promoted to the next part of our lives. But as we mature in our Christian framework, we grow in ministry servanthood and are promoted to blessing upon blessing. In order to grow and improve our spiritual life, we need to put in the work, just like my cousin needed to put in the extra time at school.

When we are elevated in the Spirit, we see more, which means that we know more. Those with the gift of prophesy see more. When you see more, you have a larger outlook on the direction and the navigation for your life. You have knowledge and insight into what's ahead because you are at a higher location. You can go further. It's called progression.

Daniel of the Old Testament knew what was needed in his life in order to be right with God (Daniel 1). He kept a kosher diet and studied the Torah. He was hated by the Babylonians because he was Jewish and because he was smart, but God blessed him with success:

> *Then the king gave Daniel high honors and many great gifts, and made him ruler over the whole province of Babylon and chief prefect over all the wise men of Babylon.*
> *—Daniel 2:48*

Daniel's court rivals successfully schemed against him so that he was thrown into the lions' den (Daniel 6), but God protected him and continued to bless him with prosperity.

If you are looking to move ahead in your spiritual life, you need to grow in your obedience to God by building a godly framework, as Daniel did. If you are doing the right thing to get promoted, then you are going to receive great gifts. Your age, your past, your social status, and your race don't matter because you have been in the presence of the Holy Spirit.

Educational principles of success also apply to promotion with God. Build a framework using the following four principles.

Listen. You have to pay attention and learn from others who have been promoted. That means you have to show up, do the homework, and get their feedback.

Study. Long hours of spiritual study involve prayer and Bible reading. You must come to the Lord when you want to, when you don't want to, when you're laughing, and when you're crying.

Attend. Go to church regularly. Hearing the Word in the presence of other believers helps you maintain your excitement and focus. When others are excited, it's easy to be excited, too.

Pay attention. You must interact mentally with what you're studying and hearing. Make connections between the things you've studied and the things you're hearing.

Benefits of Promotion

When you are promoted, you can see clearly enough to help promote others. People who are promoters promote others. Your promotion is not just for you; it's for your family and friends, as well. Your rise inspires others to work hard and seek the promotions that God has given and will give.

Spiritual disciplines are habits that draw us closer to God and provide promotional benefits. When you practice spiritual disciplines, such as reading the Bible, having daily quiet times, fasting, praying, and tithing, your focus is turned to Him, and your promotions are simply a side benefit of your relationship with God.

James 4:10 exhorts, "Humble yourselves before the Lord, and he will exalt you." This isn't just an empty promise. God will bless you if you obey Him and put in the work. Don't forget to please Him by keeping a humble heart.

What's important about promotion? It means that your framework is coming together as a solid place of refuge, service, and glory to God. It isn't just a skeleton anymore. Many believers come to faith in the Lord but don't continue to grow. They get a frame started, but they never fill in the drywall, the floors, the ceilings, the wiring, and the plumbing. Promotion is the growing of your gifts, service, and calling in the Kingdom. It's filling in your frame to the glory of God.

WORKBOOK

Chapter Thirteen Questions

Question: What is your attitude toward promotion—resistance to change, desire to do your best for God, ambition for attention and recognition, or something in between? What attitude should a Christian have toward growing in Christ?

_____
_____
_____
_____
_____
_____
_____
_____
_____
_____
_____
_____

Question: Why do some Christians never grow or mature in their faith? How can you avoid being held back?

Question: Why and how do Christians who have been promoted help promote others?

_____

_____

_____

_____

Action: What does a mature believer in Christ look like? Write a character description or draw and label a sketch with each body part described in terms of Scripture—for example, eyes that don't look at unworthy things (Psalm 101:3), ears that are quick to hear (James 1:19), and hands that serve the poor (Proverbs 31:20).

Chapter Thirteen Notes

CHAPTER FOURTEEN

In It to Win It

Jesse Owens, one of America's greatest track stars, was born in 1913. While in high school, he won three track-and-field events at the 1933 National Interscholastic Championships. Two years later, while competing for Ohio State University, he tied one world record and broke three others. Naturally, he qualified for the 1936 Olympics.

But there was a hitch. In 1936, the Olympics were held in Germany—Nazi Germany, just before what would be known as World War II. Adolf Hitler wanted the world to see how powerful and supreme the white Aryan race was in comparison to everyone else. Hitler hated America's decision to allow black athletes on the Olympic roster.

As the Olympics unfolded, it became obvious that the United States wasn't merely allowing black athletes to compete; they depended on them. Of the eleven gold medals won by the United States, six were won by African American athletes—four by Jesse Owens, who broke two world records. Reports differ, but most say that a furious Hitler stormed out of the stadium after Owens won the 100-meter dash.

When Owens returned home, he was not met by the

president, as tradition dictated, but instead by silence. Celebrating the gold medals but not his victories, Owens remained professional. "When I came back to my native country, after all the stories about Hitler, I couldn't ride in the front of the bus," he said. "I had to go to the back door. I couldn't live where I wanted. I wasn't invited to shake hands with Hitler, but I wasn't invited to the White House to shake hands with the president, either."[7]

Owens continued running and prospered financially. He raced against cars and horses, and he played with the Harlem Globetrotters. He went into public relations and marketing and set up a business in Chicago, Illinois. Owens was often called upon to speak at conventions and other business gatherings around the country. He died in March 1980.

> *I press on toward the goal for the prize of the upward call of God in Christ Jesus.*
> *—Philippians 3:14*

Why Don't I Ever Win?

Endurance is the key to winning! Building a framework isn't going to happen overnight; it's completed one little section at a time. The building process is fraught with difficulties and defeat. Some of the problems associated with failure are our own doing.

We tend to give up easily. Hopefully you, as a reader of this book, will surpass the norm and put what you've read into practice, understanding that it has the power to frame and change your life. Changing is hard, and we resist change when we're already comfortable. Jesse Owens developed an additional strategy to win in the business arena after his track career. He maintained a lifestyle of enthusiastic focus and endurance.

If you don't come up with a spiritual strategy to change and to win, you will find that you can't succeed. I am not talking about a New Year's resolution that fades out by January 12. Success typically involves lifestyle changes. Building a framework with God is for life. It's not like going on a diet, which you only follow for a short period of time. In order to make lifelong changes, we must be determined to win and devoted to winning.

Determined to Win

When you are determined, you are strong-minded or single-minded. You stand firm, no matter what. You can't allow time to wear down your winning mindset, not for an instant. Individuals who take medication understand that it wears off. You can't let your determination wear off. Be strong-minded. Pray for perseverance, but be forewarned that the answer to this prayer comes in the form of testing. In order to grow in perseverance, you need to go through difficult circumstances.

Finally, you must cut some people from your life. There are people who will undermine your determination and deplete your strength to win and succeed. The adversary has people next to you determined to take you down.

Devoted to Winning

Have the mental attitude and understanding that you matter enough to devote yourself to winning. If you are devoted, you are dedicated. Older individuals often say, "Come hell or high water." That means when the enemy comes in like a flood, you will raise the standard. Which standard? God's standard. There's no room for quitters, so if the devil causes you to doubt or tempts you to quit, you've got to tell him to get out.

If you are devoted, you are enthusiastic. You cannot

win with a losing attitude. If you are going to be devoted to winning, you must get up and pray and set your mind with a positive attitude. You must work yourself into the habits and disciplines of growing as a believer so that they become second nature to you. Think of yourself the way God thinks of you and dedicate yourself to following Him.

Obedience to God means a life of serving Him out of love and gratitude. Constantly evaluate your life to identify what is keeping you from winning. This will be a lifelong evaluation as you resist the pull to give up. This is the proof that you are a winner.

> *...not by the way of eye-service, as people-pleasers, but as bondservants of Christ, doing the will of God from the heart...*
> **—Ephesians 6:6**

Consider what framework you want for your life. What pictures and stories do you want to see when you look back and review your life? What do you want to have accomplished for God's kingdom? What did Jesse Owens see when he reviewed his accomplishments, a life lived for himself or for others? When he crossed the finish line, was it he who won or all of us?

As you focus on God, the wins will come! Winning will be inevitable if you become determined, devoted, and dependent on God.

WORKBOOK

Chapter Fourteen Questions

Question: What are some of the reasons people give up on creating and following a framework? How can you stay motivated and determined to fulfill God's plan for your life?

_____
_____
_____
_____
_____
_____
_____
_____
_____
_____
_____
_____

Question: How do you know when you need to remove someone as an influence on your life? How can you remain gracious while setting firm boundaries?

Question: How would you define winning at life? What qualities are necessary to win?

_____

_____

_____

_____

_____

Action: Imagine that you are at the end of your life, looking back. What sort of person do you want to be? What do you want to accomplish? How will you know if you have earned God's approbation, "Well done, good and faithful servant" (Matthew 25:23)? Journal about this and the changes you need to make to get there.

Chapter Fourteen Notes

CONCLUSION

A New Strategy

But my servant Caleb, because he has a different spirit and has followed me fully, I will bring into the land into which he went, and his descendants shall possess it.
—***Numbers 14:24***

In the book of Numbers, only two of the twelve spies sent into the land of Canaan had faith in God's strategy. Caleb and Joshua believed that the Israelites would enter and possess the Promised Land. The people didn't listen to Caleb and were already defeated by what faced them. They could not enter the land because of their lack of faith.

When God makes a promise, it will not fail. God promised that He would give Israel the land, but because of fear, the Israelites did not believe that it could happen. It is impossible to be defeated if God has made you a promise and assured you that He is with you, but you must have faith.

If you are not happy with where your life is heading, you may need to have a different spirit and a different strategy to achieve different results. Remember, this is not a simple New Year's resolution. You need a much more radical change, a lifestyle change.

You need to stand firm by that new strategy, by that new lifestyle, and you will win a new and successful life abundant with God's blessings. Build a framework to lead you into a life full of God's blessings!

By following God's call for our lives, we can build a framework to lead ourselves into an amazing life full of obedience and blessing. It takes hard work and discipline. We have a very real enemy pulling us away. However, if we will dedicate ourselves to moving forward one step at a time and to thinking through who God is calling us to be, we will build a framework for our lives that will ultimately shake the world to its core for Him.

Don't waste your time holding on to your past anymore. Change the language you use, address your pain and worries in a godly way, mix with the right people and situations, deal with temptations and difficulties, and listen for what God wants you to do. God has so much more for you! Begin today to build an astounding framework that will take you into God's blessed future.

Be a doer of the Word (James 1:22) and a doer of the strategies in this book. I encourage you to sit down with a journal and write out your plan for your framework. You must be intentional, or life will cause you to toss and turn every which way.

Record the private pain you need to address. Assess your associations and list ways to improve them. Decide where you will focus your thoughts, time, and activities. Set your worry, anger, and frustration at the foot of the cross. Declare your independence from sin and your dependence on God. Be intentional.

Build your own framework under the full direction of the Holy Spirit, and you will be amazed at the life God gives you!

About the Author

Dr. W. L. Bradley holds a B.S. in psychology and human services from Alabama State University; a master's degree in strategic military operations and planning and a master's degree in administration from Central Michigan University; and an Ed.D. in post-secondary education (higher education) from Argosy University. After retiring from the active U.S. Army as a lieutenant colonel, he served as assistant principal of Prattville High School and as deputy director of the Alabama Department of Transportation (Fleet Management). He is the founding pastor of Anointed Remnant International Ministries, as well as the presiding bishop of Anointed Remnant Global Assemblies. He is also the CEO of Bradley Academic and Athletic Scholarship Help, LLC. He has been married for thirty-four years and has three children, one daughter-in-law, and two grandsons.

REFERENCES

Notes

[1] "Helen Keller Biography." A & E Network. https://www.biography.com/people/helen-keller-9361967.

[2] "The Teacher Who Couldn't Read: John Corcoran's Story." TeachHUB Interview. http://www.teachhub.com/teacher-who-couldnt-read-john-corcorans-story.

[3] "Champion." Merriam-Webster. https://www.merriam-webster.com/dictionary/champion.

[4] Robinson, Glenn, III. "Sleeping with the Weights On." The Players' Tribune. April 12, 2017. https://www.theplayerstribune.com/en-us/articles/glenn-robinson-iii-indiana-pacers-dunk-contest-dad.

[5] "Mother Teresa Biography." A & E Network. https://www.biography.com/people/mother-teresa-9504160.

[6] "America's Changing Religious Landscape." Pew Research Center. May 12, 2015. https://www.pewforum.org/

2015/05/12/americas-changing-religious-landscape/.

[7] "Jesse Owens Biography." A & E Network. https://www.biography.com/people/jesse-owens-9431142.

www.ingramcontent.com/pod-product-compliance
Lightning Source LLC
Chambersburg PA
CBHW070446090426
42735CB00012B/2471